FREDERICK DOUGLASS

Abolitionist and Reformer

Rachael Phillips

BARBOUR
PUBLISHING, INC.
Uhrichsville, Ohio

Other books in the "Heroes of the Faith" series:

Brother Andrew
Gladys Aylward
Dietrich Bonhoeffer
William and Catherine Booth
John Bunyan
William Carey
Amy Carmichael
George Washington Carver
Fanny Crosby
Jonathan Edwards
Jim Elliot
Charles Finney
Billy Graham
C. S. Lewis
Eric Liddell
David Livingstone
Martin Luther
D. L. Moody

Samuel Morris
George Müller
Watchman Nee
John Newton
Florence Nightingale
Luis Palau
Francis and Edith Schaeffer
Charles Sheldon
Mary Slessor
Charles Spurgeon
John and Betty Stam
Billy Sunday
Hudson Taylor
William Tyndale
Corrie ten Boom
Mother Teresa
Sojourner Truth
John Wesley
George Whitefield

©2000 by Barbour Publishing, Inc.

ISBN 1-57748-668-4

Published by Barbour Publishing, Inc., P.O. Box 719, Uhrichsville, OH 44683
http://www.barbourbooks.com

Cover illustration © Dick Bobnick.

ecpa Member of the
Evangelical Christian
Publishers Association

Printed in the United States of America.

FREDERICK DOUGLASS

one

A shriek tore the early morning quiet into fragments that lodged painfully in seven-year-old Frederick's mind. He stirred uneasily in the rough closet that served as his bed.

"Have mercy!" begged a young woman's voice. "I won't do so no more!"

Sounds like Aunt Esther. What could be frightening her so? Frederick wiggled out of his grain sack and peered through the cracks between the boards in the closet door.

His tall, beautiful aunt stood on a bench, her hands bound tightly and fastened to one of the hooks where hams were hung. A bloody welt spanned her smooth brown shoulders that had never known her master's whip.

Until now.

Captain Aaron Anthony, known to his slaves as "Old Master," deliberately adjusted his blue cowhide, a whip made of dried ox hide that curved in the air like a scorpion's tail as he swung it again.

And again.

And again.

Frederick hugged the grain bag, crushing his thumbs into his ears; the agony of his aunt's screams and Old Master's curses clawed at him like the black swamp panther in his nightmares.

"I told you to leave that Roberts nigger* alone. Didn't I?"

"I won't never see him again!"

Crack.

"Master, please, please. . ."

Crack.

Profanity streamed from the enraged old man's mouth; the more poor Esther pleaded, the angrier he became. Frederick's skinny limbs trembled.

I'm next, he thought. *Old Master knows where I sleep.*

Days seemed to pass before the hellish song of rage and pain finally ceased. Frederick slowly raised his head. Old Master yanked Esther's limp hands down from the meat hook; the girl's slim body swayed. He shoved her out the door.

"Go work in the field today, whore! I won't have such in my kitchen!"

The old man seemed as spent as his victim. Sweat dripped from his stringy hair and sparse gray beard. He wiped the blood from the gaily-colored cowhide and limped back to his own bedroom.

Frederick lay motionless in the closet long after Old Master left the room. Even when Aunt Katy, the slave who

---

*The blatantly disparaging term "nigger" is used strictly within the historical context of this book. Its use is consistent with Mr. Douglass's quotes and those of his contemporaries. The equally disparaging terms "whore," "bastard," "white trash," "colored," and "Jim Crow" are historically accurate and appear sparingly elsewhere in the book to accurately illustrate the hostility and discrimination faced by American slaves and freedmen alike.

ran the kitchen, began to fry bacon for her master's breakfast, the small, golden-skinned boy tried to stifle his shivering breaths. Aunt Katy would not miss him if he did not appear at the large trough of cornmeal porridge on the floor where the slave children gathered like baby pigs. He would stay in his closet until Old Master, the plantation overseer, left to accompany Colonel Lloyd, the owner of the vast estate, on his morning rounds.

Frederick slipped out of the closet when he heard Aunt Katy storm down the back steps to rave at the gardener for bringing her tough collard greens. He ran to the side yard, shooing chickens away from the strawberry patch, which was his usual morning work. Even though his stomach rumbled rebelliously at the sight of the luscious red berries, he knew better than to sample any. Slaves who took fruit from Colonel Lloyd were branded as thieves. Frederick pulled the weeds out of the patch and piled them in a heap. Then he carefully swept the front yard of Old Master's house. Frederick did not want to make any mistakes today, of all days.

"Freddy, please take this message to Isaiah. I need my new shoes Thursday for the church social." Miss Lucretia, Captain Anthony's daughter, smiled at the child working so industriously.

Frederick adored Miss Lucretia; when the plantation blacksmith's son had gashed his forehead with a piece of iron, she brushed aside Aunt Katy's scolding and gently bandaged Frederick's head.

"Yes'm," answered Frederick, taking the paper.

"And," her light blue eyes twinkled at him, "this yard looks fine. I don't believe you'll have to hurry back. It is *such* a fine day."

"It is, ma'am," agreed Frederick solemnly, and scampered towards the shoemaker's hut to deliver her letter. Though thoroughly shaken by the first whipping he had ever witnessed, Frederick was still a boy. The golden Maryland sunshine promised the first good swimming of the season.

Slaves under ten rarely had to work in the fields and often gathered at Long Green, a twenty-acre meadow near the slave quarters, to play. Gray-headed women too old for heavy farm work shepherded flocks of toddlers there. The naked little ones ran like spring lambs.

Frederick had no time for babies. He would test the creek's warmth and maybe visit the windmill on Long Point, between the Miles and Wye Rivers that ran into Chesapeake Bay.

The swimming hole was as undisturbed as he had hoped. He stuck a toe in the mirrorlike water, grunting with satisfaction. A perch swam lazily at the deep end of the pool.

"Wisht I could catch you; I'm hungry enough to eat you without cookin'," said Frederick. "But I don't have nothin' for me to eat, let alone somethin' to put on a hook. So I'll just share your swimmin' hole."

He dropped the rough knee-length shirt that was his only clothing, and slid into the shallow water, feeling the winter's grime float away. The quiet pleased him. Frederick enjoyed playing with the host of slave children on Lloyd's plantation, but today he wanted to be alone with his thoughts. He missed the serenity of the forests surrounding his grandmother's cabin near the Tuckahoe River, where he had lived until last year.

Frederick Augustus Washington Bailey was born in

February 1818 on Holme Hill Farm, one of twenty or so satellite plantations owned by Colonel Edward Lloyd on the Eastern Shore of the Chesapeake Bay. It was a poor rural area with much "fever and ague," or malaria.

His mother, Harriet Bailey, was a field-worker, tall and serene-looking, with very black skin. Like many slaves, Frederick did not know who his father was; he knew only that he was a white man. He had heard old Bessie and Emma chattering the other night, unaware of his presence outside the slave quarters. He hovered near the door after his meager supper, hoping for the extra piece of cornbread the old women often gave him.

"Don't eat them berries, I done set them by for Freddy," scolded Bessie.

"Poor little feller, he hungry all the time," assented Emma.

"He Old Master's baby, don't you know?" confided Bessie.

" 'Course I do; don't ev'rybody? . . ."

Frederick had broken into a run; not even the berries were enough to make him stay. It was by no means the first time he had heard the rumor that Captain Anthony was his father, but he did not have to listen to it. He did not want to listen to it, or think about it. Especially now.

Instead, he would sit under the green willows' long, comforting arms, and remember his grandmother, Betsey Bailey. It was she, rather than his mother, who had cared for him ever since he could remember. She did not live in the slave quarters on the farm, as Frederick's mother did. Her cabin, surrounded by loblolly pines, had a dirt floor and no windows. Frederick, his cousins, and his Uncle Henry, who was two years younger than Frederick, played endless games on the loft ladder, scrambling with the agility of young squirrels while Grandmammy laughed. She often sent them outside with her daughter Priscilla to fish for shad and herring in the creek. Frederick liked to visit Mr. Lee's mill, where he could watch the huge wheel turn. He drew his own drink from the well in Grandmammy's yard.

Grandmammy was special, Frederick knew. She was paid as a midwife to the young slaves. She sold wonderful fishing nets to people as far away as Denton and Hillsboro, and was permitted to keep some of the money. She was famous, too, for her seed sweet potatoes. Folks were convinced if Grandmammy just touched their taters before they planted them, they would have a bumper crop!

But as Frederick grew, Grandmammy told him that when he got big, he would go to live with Old Master. Old Master owned this land, this cabin, the well, and even herself. Old Master also owned Frederick and would some day send for him. Frederick feared growing taller, and even tried to eat a little less, hoping he could stay with Grandmammy.

Early one summer morning when Frederick was six, Grandmammy put on her freshly ironed turban and told him they were going on a long walk together. She did not tell him their destination. When Frederick's legs gave out, his grandmother picked him up and carried him effortlessly for long distances. She was "marvelously straight in figure, elastic, and muscular," wrote Frederick later. "She would have 'toted' me farther, but that I felt myself too much of a man to allow it, and insisted on walking."[1] Frederick was not too grown up to cling to her, however, when they entered a dark forest where the dead logs appeared to be monsters that would eat him alive. Grandmammy reassured him that the "eyes were knots, washed white with rain, the legs were broken limbs, and the ears, only ears owing to the point from which they were seen. Thus early I learned that the point from which a thing is viewed is of some importance."[2]

They finally arrived at Colonel Edward Lloyd's plantation in the sweltering heat of late afternoon. Frederick found himself surrounded by a crowd of black, brown, copper-colored, and nearly white slave children. The fields, too, teemed with adult slaves, both male and female. The plantation was far noisier than the woods at Tuckahoe.

"Look, there's your cousins! And there," Grandmammy smiled sadly, "is your brother Perry. See how big he is!" Eleven-year-old Perry grinned at Frederick. His sisters Sarah, ten, and Eliza, eight, were glad to see Grandmammy again, and welcomed Frederick. He stared at them curiously. He had never seen his siblings before. "Brothers and sisters we were by blood," said Frederick later, "but slavery had made us strangers."[3]

Grandmammy hugged all of her grandchildren. "Go play! And take Freddy with y'all!"

But Frederick had held tightly to his grandmother's skirts. Gently she detached his small fingers. "I'm gonna visit with Maisie," she smiled at the wrinkled old woman who was supervising the children, "and rest a spell. You be a good boy, Frederick." Grandmammy caressed his face with a hand as soft as worn calico. "It's fixin' to storm. Y'all go play in the back room."

Reluctantly, Frederick followed the group to a huge room in the slave quarters where they ran joyously and played games. He backed against a wall to watch.

"Fed, Fed! Grandmammy gone! Grandmammy gone!" chanted a mischievous voice. Jerry, his cousin, danced in front of him.

Terrified, Frederick ran back to the kitchen. It was true! His grandmother had disappeared.

"No! No!" screamed Frederick. How could his own

grandmammy lie to him?

"Give him them peaches," said Maisie, with a practiced air.

"Here, Freddy," said Perry, holding out two plump peaches, a perfect treat rarely given to slaves.

Frederick struck them to the floor, and the other children swarmed like minnows to grab the fruit. He ran blindly to a dark corner in the kitchen, where he huddled, crying, until he fell asleep, worn out by the long walk and loneliness.

Eventually Frederick realized that he would have to accept his new life if he was going to survive. He even learned to like some aspects of it.

"But I wish I was back at Grandmammy's," Frederick told the two blackbirds that perched inquisitively on a dead stump. "I wish I was free, like you!" he called, as they flew away.

At first Frederick had been terrified of encountering the Old Master. To his surprise, several days passed before he saw Captain Anthony. Frederick stayed in the slave quarters until he was summoned to Old Master's large, red-brick house.

Charlie, who accompanied him, pushed Frederick through the kitchen door. "Here's yo' new one, Aunt Katy," he said.

" 'Nother one to feed," said the woman sourly, her dark face wrinkling with distaste. "You know how to snap beans? Well, you take this here dishpan out back and do it." Her virulent brown eyes regarded him like a hostile dog's. "And don't you think of eatin' any. Them's for Old Master. I'll skin you alive if even one's missin'. Now, git!"

Frederick was only too glad to leave. Other boys and girls in the yard worked at their morning tasks, too busy to notice Frederick. He was glad to remain anonymous, sitting in the shade of the big locust tree.

"Old Master comin'!" The tallest boy, who had stopped for a few moments to wipe his wet forehead, began to hoe furiously. The others quickly followed suit. Frederick froze, unable to make his fingers break the green beans into pieces. *Work!* said his panicked brain. *Work! Old Master comin'!* But his small hands refused to move.

The old man was nothing like the devils Frederick had imagined. He had large, empty eyes and scraggly gray hair. He appeared to be muttering to himself.

"He ain't gonna get away with it," said Old Master.

He leaned on his walking stick, passing through the group of slave children as if they were a flock of geese.

"He'll find out!" growled Old Master as he slammed the front door behind him.

The children all breathed a sigh of relief.

"Old Master used to be the captain of Colonel Lloyd's sloop over on the river," explained Sammy, the tall boy. "He been head overseer for years, they say. But now he actin' strange sometimes; thinks people nobody can see is out to get him. We jes' try to stay out of his way."

Frederick nodded gratefully. In the days to come, he learned to discern Old Master's worst moods coming on; if the old man started shaking his head and snapping his fingers, it was an immediate signal to make oneself scarce. Any offense, real or imagined, was magnified a thousand times when he was in that frame of mind.

At times, the old gentleman was almost kind; one day Captain Anthony actually patted Frederick on the head, calling him his "little Indian boy."

He was glad that Old Master mostly ignored the slave children he owned. In a way, the child pitied the unhappy old man who seemed at war with himself.

Until now.

God, who lived way up in the sky, was good, Frederick had been told. He made everyone; He made white people to be masters and black people to be slaves. He knew what was best for everybody.[4]

"But it was not good!" Frederick cried. "It was not good that Old Master whipped poor Esther and made her scream!" Beautiful Esther, with her ripe-blackberry eyes and musical laugh, who told Frederick and the other children stories when Aunt Katy was off cursing somebody—it was not good that the Old Master should hurt Esther!

Besides, thought Frederick, *how did people know that God made black people to be slaves? Did they go up in the sky and learn it? Or did He come down and tell them so?*[5]

The little boy swam round the silent pool. As the sun floated higher in the sky, Frederick climbed out and put on his dirty shirt once more. He headed back for Old Master's house so that Aunt Katy could not use his being late as an excuse for withholding his noon cornbread. Frederick's small mind was no more peaceful than when he had arrived at his refuge.

"I never shall forget it [the whipping] whilst I remember anything," Frederick later wrote in his first autobiography. "It was the first of a long series of such outrages, of which I was doomed to be a witness and a participant. It struck me with awful force. It was the bloodstained gate, the entrance to the hell of slavery, through which I was about to pass."[6]

two

"Time to go huntin', Fed!"

Frederick followed Daniel, the youngest son of Colonel Lloyd, through the village of kitchens, washhouses, dairies, barns, and craftsmen's huts behind the Great House. Hundreds of black slaves labored daily to make the Lloyd plantation self-sufficient.

Frederick waved to a few of his playmates; they stared enviously at him. To be companion to Master Daniel from the Great House was indeed an honor, and exempted one from hauling wood or fetching water. Frederick knew he was taller and stronger than most children his age; his golden color also set him apart. But even he sometimes wondered why those at the Great House chose their chief overseer's six-year-old slave to accompany their twelve-year-old son around the plantation.

"Gore comin'," said Daniel in a low voice.

It was as if the sun had suddenly gone out. The cheerful morning noises continued, even accelerated. Tony, the blacksmith, pounded his glowing horseshoe as if to smash it in two. Cilla and Lucy scrubbed long underwear with fervor.

Mr. Gore, an overseer, walked among the shacks, his sharp black eyes darting from slave to slave. They rarely heard his high, piercing voice. They often felt his whip.

Andy, a carpenter's apprentice, stared at the wood he was planing with quiet hatred. Two years before, Mr. Gore had chased his brother into a creek, vowing to whip him. Denby had refused to leave the creek when ordered.

"If you're not on your knees here by the time I count three, I'll kill you," Mr. Gore had said.

Denby simply waded farther into the creek.

"One. . .two. . .three." A shot rang out, and the young man sank below the surface of the water in a fountain of blood.

Mr. Gore had cleaned his gun, and ordered the horrified blacks back to their work.

The entire plantation rocked with the news. Cruelty, even barbarity, was common. The Great Farm had been known for generations for its unusually harsh treatment of its slaves. But most healthy blacks knew they presented economic value, if not human value, to their master. He would not allow his expensive property abused to the point of losing it.

But Denby's death destroyed that fragile web of security.

Old Master, Frederick knew, had protested angrily to Colonel Lloyd. As head overseer, he detested this young fool's recklessness.

Gore had answered coolly that if one slave refused to be corrected, then all of them would follow his example. Soon all slaves would rebel against their masters, and the whites themselves would become slaves.

Such logic seemed to satisfy Colonel Lloyd. Mr. Gore and his pitiless whip remained.

Now he paused in front of the boys. Frederick sucked his breath in as he had when the boys had encountered a rattlesnake in the swamp.

"Good morning, Master Daniel."

"Morning, Mr. Gore."

"Good luck with your hunting." He turned toward the barns.

The boys slowly exhaled.

The Great House is a pleasure to look at, Frederick thought. It was an enormous, dignified white building with three wings and a portico supported by stately white columns. A summerhouse, greenhouses full of exotic plants, vine-covered arbors, and shady old trees surrounded the mansion.

Frederick's friend Bessie sometimes spoke of a wonderful place a long time ago called the Garden of Eden where the flowers always bloomed and animals were unafraid. *It must have looked something like Colonel Lloyd's front yard,* thought Frederick.

A luxurious carriage passed through the ornate black iron gate and made its way to the Great House. Wilks, the light-skinned coachman, helped an elderly lady in a voluminous lavender dress and large feathered hat out of the carriage.

"Run!" hissed Daniel. "Head for the fields!"

The two did not slow until they could hear the songs of field hands clearing brush next to the tobacco fields.

"Why were we running so fast?" asked Frederick.

"Great-aunt Virginia," panted Daniel. "She has come for my birthday celebration tomorrow. If she spotted me now, we would never get away to hunt. She'd kiss me and call me a 'little gentleman.' Then I'd have to play my violin for her and read her the catechism all day." Daniel shuddered.

Frederick felt true sympathy for his friend, although he doubted that Aunt Virginia could hold a candle to Aunt Katy.

"That coachman," said Frederick, "he do look just like Master Murray, don't he?"

Daniel suddenly loomed over him. "Never say that, never, do you hear me? Murray will have you whipped, or at least sent away. My brother won't stand to be compared to him. Just keep your mouth shut, and you and me can go on hunting and fishing. Promise, Fed."

Frederick promised to die before he would ever say it again, and Daniel relaxed.

"Birthdays aren't all bad, even if you have to put on a suit with a bow tie and have your kinfolks to dinner." He grinned. "I can have anything I want for my birthday dinner."

"Anything?" asked Frederick, awestruck at the thought. "I'd have fried chicken like Old Master eats for Sunday dinner. Maybe even two pieces."

Daniel laughed. "I already told Albert I want partridge, oysters, Spanish grapes, and plum pudding. And we always bring out the silver—pounds and pounds of it—for birthdays, along with lots of crystal. The dining room looks like a pirate's treasure cave in the firelight. Father said he would get me a new gun for my birthday. This thing is too tiny for a thirteen-year-old." He swaggered, a little like the Colonel.

Daniel did not ask him his birthday, and Frederick could not have told him if he had wanted to.

They both knew that slaves did not have birthdays.

The wake-up horn was earlier than usual, realized Frederick, as he emerged from his grain bag, rubbing his cold feet. It was February—time to get the fields ready for planting. A stream of shivering slaves, some of them young women with babies tied to their backs, erupted from the slave quarters. They headed for the fields, each fighting to get ahead of the others, as the last field hand emerging always received a whack from the overseer's heavy oak stick.

"Fed! Go get wood for the fire. Phil, Jerry, you go, too. Ain't no breakfast for nobody till this fire gets built."

Frederick obediently headed for the woodpile. Phil and Jerry, Aunt Katy's sons, jostled Frederick until he lost his grip on his small load. The logs crashed to the ground. Enraged, Frederick struck Jerry with his fist. Phil bawled for their mother, and Aunt Katy emerged from the back door to find Frederick and Phil swinging furiously at each other. She grabbed Frederick by the neck of his shirt and shook him like an errant puppy.

"You! When you goin' quit actin' like white trash!"

"Mama, he hurt Jerry—"

"Git in the house! I don' want to hear nothin' about it!"

Aunt Katy had once gouged Phil's arm with a knife, so he knew better than to argue with her. He and Jerry disappeared inside the kitchen door.

"You ain't worth feedin', you hear me? Stay out here on the woodpile. I don' want to hear a sound from you!" Aunt Katy spun Frederick into the wall and raged back into the house.

Frederick lay bruised and hungry; he would miss breakfast, he knew, but Aunt Katy usually forgot about him by lunchtime. He could always sneak off later to search for oysters down by the riverbeds. Sometimes he sang outside Miss Lucretia's window, and she gave him a slice of bread and butter. Mas' Daniel was gone to visit his cousins downriver, so there was no chance for a treat from him. But Bessie and Emma were good for a handout if he got desperate. Having weathered Aunt Katy's storms for well over a year, Frederick had created his own system of survival.

But after breakfast, Aunt Katy stuck her head out the door.

"You! Git in here and scour these pots! They'd better be shinin' clean, or I'll whip your tail till it bleeds, you hear me?"

Scrubbing the heavy black kettles was a chore usually assigned to older children. Frederick rubbed their rough surfaces with sand, then scrubbed them with the harsh lye soap that wore his skin down till it tore like paper. It was going to be a long morning.

"Aunt Katy—"

"You think you goin' get cornbread like the others? I don't feed no cornbread to chilluns that fight like white trash. Git!"

Frederick burst into tears as he ran from the kitchen. Aunt Katy had kept him working all day, giving him no chance to use his alternative food sources. While he toiled, Frederick could smell the luscious fragrance of Old Master's favorite huckleberry pie. His stomach clung to his backbone like a dried-up pea pod on a vine.

An old hound wandered into the yard. Frederick poured out his misery to the droopy-eared animal, hugging him close in the twilight. The dog nosed him sympathetically, and Frederick felt a little comforted. Maybe he could sneak into the kitchen and steal a crumb or two if Aunt Katy visited the slave quarters after supper. He was too exhausted to venture out in the dark to find food.

Sure enough, Katy emerged from the kitchen and strode away. Frederick waited until she disappeared, then slipped into the house. The pantry was locked securely, as he had expected. But Frederick spied a dried-up ear of

Indian corn under the table. He rubbed the kernels from the cob and wrapped them in wet oak leaves from the front yard. Frederick took the small packet to the fireplace and covered it with glowing ashes. He stuck his tired feet close to the warmth. If only Aunt Katy would talk on and on like she usually did. . .

What was that? Frederick knew he had been dozing. A tall woman materialized in front of him, and he shrank back in terror. But the phantom did not strike him. Instead, she picked him up with large, gentle hands and held him close to her heart.

"Freddy, don't be afraid," said Frederick's mother.

Frederick stared in delight. He remembered seeing his mother only a few times since he was born. But he had never forgotten her. Harriet Bailey was serene and stately with the high cheekbones, straight nose, and broad forehead that spoke of her Barbados background. Unlike most slaves, she could read. Her shining, midnight-black face glowed with the joy of holding her son. Harriet had walked twelve miles from Mr. Stewart's plantation, where Old Master had hired her out.

"You are so growed! Let me look at you!"

As Harriet examined Frederick, her dark brows met pointedly.

"Where you get them bruises? Why you got blood on your head? You ain't in trouble with Old Master, are you?"

"No, Mama, but—"

"But what?"

"Can I get my corn out of the fireplace? I'm awful hungry."

"Sure, child. Is that all you eat this evenin'?"

"Yes, Mama. It's all I eat all day."

"Harriet!" Aunt Katy paused at the door in unbelief.

"Yes," said Frederick's mother evenly, "I come to visit. Sit down. I got somethin' to say to you."

Aunt Katy did not want to visit, but Harriet blocked the door, her black eyes glowing, her white teeth glistening in a predatory smile. She was much bigger than her cousin. So Aunt Katy sat down.

Harriet drew Frederick to her lap and encircled him with warm arms. He munched his Indian corn, enjoying his view of Aunt Katy's discomfiture.

"You listen to me," said Harriet, her smile disappearing. "My boy is skinny, and he say he had nothin' to eat today. He beat up. This how you run a kitchen? This how you take care of Old Master's slaves? Old Master mean sometimes, but he don't cotton to one slave beatin' up another. He'll whip you good if I tell him. You know he will. So you better feed Frederick, and if you lay a hand on him, I'll come some night, and we'll talk again." Harriet grasped the smaller woman's wrist tightly until she winced. "Now, get out."

Aunt Katy scuttled out like a frightened roach.

Frederick's mother turned to him with a smile. "I got a surprise for you, my valentine." She unwrapped a large, glazed cake in the shape of a heart. Frederick had never seen such a treat, let alone eaten one. He felt like a king, savoring the delicious flavor, seated on his mother's lap. Harriet sang and told Frederick stories. "That night I learned the fact that I was not only a child, but *somebody's* child," Frederick wrote later.[1]

He fell asleep in heaven, but woke up in Aunt Katy's kitchen. Frederick's mother was nowhere to be seen. She had to walk the twelve miles back to Mr. Stewart's plantation before the wake-up horn sounded in order to avoid a beating herself.

Aunt Katy did not deprive him of food for a while, and

she refrained from extreme physical abuse. But the safety he enjoyed vanished several months later when Aunt Katy told Frederick that his mother had caught a bad illness and died.

"I am going away to the Great House Farm!
  O yea! O yea!"
The rich melody resounded throughout the tobacco field as the field hands cultivated the young plants. One group sang out the melody, and another answered with the plaintive echo, "O yea! O yea!" Many slave owners pointed to the workers' songs as evidence of their happiness in slavery. But young as Frederick was, he detected the truth. Slaves' songs were an emotional release from their sufferings. "Slaves sing most when they are most unhappy," Douglass wrote later. "Every tone was a testimony against slavery, and a prayer to God for deliverance from chains."[2]

Anderson, the field overseer, flicked his bright green whip idly and scanned the tobacco rows once more. Whether the slaves were happy or sad made no difference to him. He liked their singing because it helped him keep track of where they were. A quiet slave, he reasoned, was trouble.

Frederick waved to his brother, Perry, who, at thirteen, was considered big enough to work in the fields. Perry smiled at Frederick, but he knew better than to draw attention to himself. Sweat poured from his forehead, dripped from his broad young chest. Frederick watched sadly as Perry hoed. No more carefree mornings playing tag on Long Green for Perry. For the rest of his life he would toil in his master's fields, unpaid and unnoticed, except when the overseer would whip him for working too slow. Frederick turned away.

"I'll see if Mas' Daniel wants me this morning," thought Frederick. He made his way back towards the Great House, choosing the way by the stables. He hoped to sneak past the vigilant grooms and pet a velvety nose. Colonel Lloyd's horses were all thoroughbreds; he was as particular about his horses and pack of thirty pedigreed hounds as he was about his family. The animals had the finest quarters possible and were fed far better than the slaves. Frederick loved to watch the hunts that were a regular part of plantation life during the cool months.

But Colonel Lloyd himself stood before the stable door with Old Barney. He was a tall, well-built man with striking, prematurely white hair and blue eyes that won over peer and slave alike. He was an immensely wealthy, shrewd politician who eventually served three times as governor of Maryland and twice as a U.S. Senator. Colonel Lloyd was a kind husband and father and a generous host to a constant stream of company—more guests, it was said, than patronized the local hotels. But now the eyes were blue ice, his face wooden and implacable.

"This horse has not been taken care of properly," said the Colonel. "He has been given too much hay, and that too late in the day. No wonder he is ill. A fool would know better than to treat him this way. Take off your jacket and kneel, you old rascal!"

Old Barney, a bald, portly black man who had cared for his master's horses for thirty years, knew the sick horse had contracted a disease that had nothing to do with his diet. But he could not reply. It was not allowed. He took off his jacket slowly and knelt in the dust. His son, Young Barney, who assisted him in the stable, stood helplessly as Colonel Lloyd wielded his whip.

Crack.

24

Crack.

Crack.

The old man groaned. . . .

Run! Frederick thought. But his feet would not obey, and he stood watching until the elderly groom fell over on the ground.

"Take him away," said Colonel Lloyd. "Keep him out of the stables until I call for him. Perhaps he has learned not to neglect a good horse."

Frederick finally ducked behind a wagon. Then he ran, tears rolling down his cheeks, chest heaving, into the woods until he could run no more. He screamed until his voice was hoarse. Years later, Frederick could not forget the scene: "Here were two men, both advanced in years; there were the silvery locks of Colonel Lloyd, and there was the bald and toilworn brow of Old Barney; master and slave; superior and inferior here, but *equals* at the bar of God."[3]

Frederick lay quietly on his back, marveling at the serene blue sky that smiled so when everything else was in pain. Uncle Noah and Aunt Jenny, he had heard, escaped from Old Master and ran away up North! Frederick had never heard of such a thing. Bessie and the other slaves discussed their flight in whispers. It seemed at the time a curiosity not to be believed, like snow in September. But now he felt a fierce gladness that his relatives had fled from a plantation where faithful old servants could be beaten at the whim of a white man.

Old Master had sold Noah and Jenny's small children down South in revenge for the escape, as well as Frederick's Aunt Maryann and cousin Betsy. They were doomed to mistreatment and early deaths from overwork in the sugar cane and cotton fields of Mississippi, Louisiana, and Alabama.

"I will escape," said Frederick in a whisper to the smiling sky. "I will."

"Fed, where on earth have you been?" asked Miss Lucretia. "I was hopin' for a song from you."

Frederick tried to grin, but could not do it, not even for Miss Lucretia.

"Some days just aren't meant for songs, is that it?"

Frederick nodded.

"Well, you don't have to sing for me right now. Sit there and eat this bread and butter while I tell you something! Father has decided to send you to my husband's brother's home in Baltimore. They need an able boy to help take care of his son, run errands, and do chores. We thought you fit the bill exactly."

Frederick stared in disbelief. The heavenly slice of bread went unheeded for a few moments. He had heard from his older cousin Tom that Baltimore was far grander than anything on the plantation. There were huge ships four times as big as Colonel Lloyd's sloops. Baltimore!

"When am I leaving?" said Frederick, when he finally found the words.

"In three days," said Miss Lucretia, pleased to see the sparkle in the little boy's listless eyes. "But you will have to be very clean there. I understand that folks in Baltimore expect their servants to be spotless. If you get rid of all that grime, I shall make you a pair of trousers."

Frederick was speechless. He had never worn trousers in his life! Without another word, he ran to the creek, where he spent the better part of the next three days scrubbing himself.

"I may be deemed superstitious and egotistical, in regarding this event as a special interposition of Divine Providence in my favor," wrote Douglass in his autobiography *My*

26

Bondage and My Freedom. "I should be false to the earliest and most cherished sentiments of my soul, if I suppressed or hesitated to avow that opinion, although it may be characterized as irrational by the wise, and ridiculous by the scoffer . . .slavery would not always be able to hold me within its foul embrace; and this conviction, like a word of living faith, strengthened me through the darkest trials of my lot. This good spirit was from God; and to Him I offer thanksgiving and praise."[4]

three

Y'all wake up," said a deep voice beside Frederick. "We's in Baltimore, and we got to get this cargo and you to the right places."

He opened his eyes to see Rich, a friendly deckhand, grin at him.

Frederick scrambled to his feet. The trip on the plantation sloop *Sally Lloyd* had stirred his imagination: sailors deftly guiding the boat on the Miles River; sea vessels with their white sails blowing in the Chesapeake Bay breeze; Annapolis with its elegant domed state capitol. And now, Baltimore!

The sloop docked at Smith Wharf in the heart of the city's busy mercantile shipping center.

"Grab that lamb!" yelled Rich. "We got to get them sheep to Mr. Curtis's slaughterhouse before we take you to Mr. Auld's."

The lamb was a yearling; he was strong, and he had his own ideas about going to the slaughterhouse. Frederick tugged and yelled like all the deckhands as they drove the sheep down Pratt Street.

"Got that done," Rich sighed with relief, as they returned to the *Sally Lloyd*. "Now wash yo' hands and face. Y'all don't want Miss Sophia to see a dirty little Eastern Shoreman come to her door!"

Frederick scrubbed himself fiercely, then followed Rich through the streets of Baltimore, so amazed that he sometimes forgot to put one foot in front of the other. The city was awake now; church bells rang from every direction. Frederick wanted to stand, closing his eyes and absorbing the grandeur. Instead, he and Rich joined hundreds of pedestrians on their way to church, dodging carriages full of beautifully dressed men, women, and children. Frederick marveled at the warm cloaks and greatcoats that even the poorest people owned.

"Child," said Rich with exasperation. "We so slow it gonna be evenin' before we reach Mr. Hugh's. Why you gotta stop like a mule every two steps?"

"Rich," breathed Frederick, "look."

A mahogany-colored man dressed impeccably in a black suit held the arm of an attractive woman in a rich wine-colored dress and bonnet. Their children trailed behind them, little girls in ruffled pantalets and Sunday dresses, boys uncomfortably stylish in knickers with large bows under their chins.

"Rich," whispered Frederick, "I ain't never seen no Negroes with shoes before. They's *hundreds* of 'em."

Rich smiled at the youngster. "Mebbe Miss Sophia get you shoes one of these days. If you's good, that is."

Frederick's bare, brown toes were suddenly an embarrassment. He had not seen any child wearing the long cotton shirt that was the standard uniform for slaves, either. How kind Miss Lucretia was to make him the new nut-brown trousers! Shoes would probably be uncomfortable at first, like the trousers, but Frederick wanted to look like a native of Baltimore.

"I'll be the best help Miss Sophia ever had," he declared.

"Then let's stop the dawdlin' and get there."

Rich and Frederick made their way through the streets past thousands of houses, it seemed to Frederick. How did a person find one house among the rows? It was like trying to find one special tobacco plant in a field.

The two arrived at a two-story house on the corner of Aliceanna Street and Happy Alley in a shabby but respectable area of Baltimore called Fells Point, where all the men were employed in the shipbuilding industry. Rich knocked at the back door, and a young woman opened it, beaming, a rosy little boy peeping out from behind her skirts.

"You are Frederick," said Sophia Auld. "Your feet must be freezing! Come in, child, warm yourself by the fire. Rich, would you like a cup of tea?"

Rich had to give Frederick a shove. *Miss Lucretia was kind to me,* thought Frederick, *but she never looked me right in the eye like that.* He was overwhelmed with gratitude and confusion. Staring a white person straight in the face was an unforgivable sin that warranted a lashing. Frederick huddled by the fire and accepted a cup of milk from his mistress, wide-eyed at such a treat.

The toddler edged closer to Frederick, studying him with inquisitive eyes.

"That is your Freddy," said Miss Sophia. "Freddy will take good care of you, Tommy." The little one hugged Frederick with chubby, dimpled arms.

"You must be very kind to Tommy, Freddy," said Miss Sophia.

Frederick, who was joyously aghast at his first hug from a white person, nodded vigorously, unable to speak.

Rich drained his cup and bowed to Miss Sophia.

"Must get back to the boat," he said. "Be a good boy, Fed."

Frederick watched in wonder as Miss Sophia washed cups and plates, made biscuits, and stirred beans simmering in a big black kettle. Miss Lucretia often sewed needlework or made clothes for the family, but she never did kitchen chores. He could hardly believe that the busy hands belonged to a white woman.

He did not know that Sophia, before her marriage, had been a weaver who earned her own living. Most women in the South were either slave owners' wives, servants, or slaves. Sophia was part of a budding middle class that did not know how to issue orders or frighten servants into obedience.

"Did you like the boat ride?" asked Miss Sophia, stacking dishes. "Keep Tommy away from the fire. Had you ever been on a boat before?"

"Y–yes," answered Frederick, edging the little boy away from danger. "I love to watch the big ships with their sails all flying in the wind."

"We'll have to make a trip down to the wharves one day, you and I and Tommy," said Miss Sophia. "Ships from all over the world dock there—there are piles of the most interesting things: coffee beans, strange fruits and vegetables, jugs of molasses—rum, too, I'm sure." She clacked her tongue disapprovingly. "We'll avoid The Hook, of course. That is an evil, sinful place." She brightened. "But the docks are a wonderful place to visit."

"Yes'm," said Frederick.

Frederick tickled Tommy under his chin and made silly faces for him. But a part of him sat mesmerized, unable to believe that Miss Sophia was calmly talking as if he were a real person. It was the most amazing afternoon he had ever spent.

"Mr. Auld will soon be home," said Miss Sophia. "Please get us some more firewood. Then wash your hands and set the table."

Frederick fetched the logs, giving a small stick to Tommy so he could "help." "Don't run with that," he instructed his small assistant. "Give it to me so I can put it in the fire. No, you can't do that, Tommy. Give it to me. That's right. Now, let's wash our hands, and we'll put the tin cups on the table."

Sophia Auld smiled thankfully, watching Frederick handle her son with surprising ease. Freddy was everything she had hoped for—beautiful, intelligent, and sweet-tempered. Lucretia had written that he had served as a companion for the youngest Lloyd boy. *That must be where he got that accent,* Sophia thought. *The child sounds like no plantation slave I ever heard. He won't look at me, though. Did I frighten him somehow?*

Aloud, she said, "Freddy?"

"Yes, Miss Sophia?"

"Look at me, Freddy. Look *up,* child. Are you scared of me?"

Frederick's face broke into the biggest grin ever. "No'm, I ain't."

"Good," smiled Sophia. "I want you to be happy here."

"Yes'm," agreed Frederick, looking straight into her eyes.

The day was a continual revelation to Frederick. When he found he was expected to eat meals with the Aulds, he was terrified. This would be so different from Aunt Katy's trough of mush on the floor! But he watched Miss Sophia closely and enjoyed the steaming bean soup (with salt pork in it, yet!) and crisp cornbread spread with sweet butter.

Hugh Auld was silent throughout the meal. Occasionally he looked up from his plate to catch his wife's eye or chuckle at his son's antics. He nodded at Frederick when Sophia introduced him, but did not appear to notice much. That was fine. The fact that Miss Sophia and Tommy loved Frederick was enough.

Bedtime was even more startling. Frederick had already chosen a warm sleeping spot in the kitchen: a small closet next to the fireplace. Eventually he would find another grain bag to cover him, but Frederick still thought it a good place.

He washed the supper dishes, then helped Miss Sophia get Tommy ready for bed. He sang Tommy to sleep in his trundle bed.

"You have a magic voice, Freddy," said Miss Sophia. "He never stays in his bed without my being there."

They entered the hallway. "Your room is this way," directed Miss Sophia.

"My room?" said Frederick.

"We'll see you in the morning," said Miss Sophia. She patted his cheek gently. "Sweet dreams."

Frederick opened the door hesitatingly and surveyed the tiny cubicle. A small bed with a plump straw mattress, clean sheets and colorful quilt, and a tin washbasin and pitcher on a miniature table furnished his room. His very own room.

Frederick had never slept in a bed, so the sheets were a puzzle. But it made no sense to get on top of them or get under them; surely, one was to get between them. He crept into the bed. A light shower began falling outside. His normally cold toes grasped the bedcovers appreciatively.

"Sweet dreams," Miss Sophia said, thought Frederick. *I can't think of any dream sweeter than this, other than my*

mama coming back for me. I hope this ain't a dream. If it is, I don't want to wake up.

The first few weeks in Baltimore were sometimes difficult for Frederick. When he took his pail to the pump on Washington Street to fetch the Aulds' morning water, the thunderous rumble of wagons through the narrow cobblestoned streets stopped him dead in his tracks.

"Look sharp," yelled a driver who swerved to miss the staring boy. "Haven't you ever seen a horse before?"

Worse yet, gangs of adolescent white boys wandered the streets. More than once Frederick returned from doing errands for Miss Sophia with his heart pounding, his face dripping with sweat.

"Eastern Shoreman! Eastern Shoreman!" the boys taunted him.

Sometimes Frederick craved the solitude of his swimming hole, the summer greenness of the plantation.

But not for long.

He reveled in being "Freddy" instead of "Old Master's Fed."

He loved his whole set of new clothes that made him look like the other boys in his neighborhood. The shoes were not so bad, once a fellow got used to them.

He relished mealtimes; Frederick even had fried chicken with the Aulds on Sundays.

Baltimore continued to stir Frederick's imagination. The wharves, the shipbuilding yards, the launching of each proud new frigate with pomp and pageantry—it was paradise for a boy.

Best of all, Frederick enjoyed the novel sense of everyday affection he experienced in the Auld household. Tommy adored Frederick, and he learned to care for the little boy

34

deeply. Miss Sophia was not Frederick's mother; she was still his master's wife. But her many kindnesses warmed the love-starved child. He had not felt so cherished since his days with Grandmammy Bailey in her cabin on Tuckahoe Creek.

Miss Sophia was the daughter of strict Methodists. Her husband had little interest in such things; so when he worked late, Miss Sophia often read aloud from the Bible in her parlor. Tommy and the new baby, Ann Elizabeth, were already in bed, but Frederick begged to stay up a little longer. She consented with a smile, and began reading in the book of Job:

Where wast thou when I laid the foundations of
the earth? declare, if thou hast understanding.
Who hath laid the measures thereof, if thou know-
est? or who hath stretched the line upon it?
Whereupon are the foundations thereof fastened?
or who laid the corner stone thereof; When the
morning stars sang together, and all the sons of
God shouted for joy? (Job 38:4–7)

I never heard such wonderful, grand words before, thought Frederick. The rhythm and beauty of the Scriptures seemed to move his very being, even though he understood little of the King James English. He was intrigued, too, with the trail of tiny black marks on a page that said so much.

Frederick waited, motionless, until Miss Sophia had finished. He crept up to his mistress, touched the Bible reverently with one finger, and asked, "Miss Sophia, is this God's book?"

"Why, yes, it certainly is," said Mrs. Auld.

"And God tells us what He wants us to know in this book?"

"Yes, Freddy."

"Miss Sophia, I really would love to learn to read God's book like you."

Sophia Auld's eyes filled with tears. "Of course, you shall, Freddy," she answered. "God wants us all to know what His book says."

She began to teach Frederick the first few letters of the alphabet every night when Hugh was absent. Together they pored over the Old Testament. Frederick was overwhelmed. There were so many a's and b's in the Bible! But he persevered. Within a month Frederick could read a few two- and three-letter words. His teacher was almost as excited as he was.

"We must tell Mr. Auld of your remarkable progress!" exulted Sophia. "Let's show him tonight!"

So that evening, after Hugh's favorite clam chowder, Sophia announced that she and Freddy had a surprise. Hugh grunted agreeably and sat near the fire, smiling to see his young, pretty wife so animated. She smiled encouragingly, and Frederick stood tall and proud to read.

"B-a-d, bad. H-a-d, had. L-a-d, lad. M-a-d—"

Frederick got no farther, as Hugh grabbed the paper from him and tore it into a hundred pieces. Sophia froze like a frightened rabbit, her eyes dark with questions. Frederick felt a hot burn of shame and anger rising in his body.

"What are you thinking of, Sophia, to teach a slave how to read!" shouted Hugh. "Have you lost your mind completely, woman?"

Sophia crumpled like a crushed flower. "I–I only wanted to teach him to read the Bible," she answered softly. "I thought everyone should know about God."

"Don't you know that if you teach that one to read the Bible, there will be no stopping him?" raged Hugh. "He'll be unhappy as a slave, and the first thing you know, he'll try to run away! Besides, it's against the law to teach a slave to read. I won't have any such goings-on in my house, Sophia. Promise me that you'll keep Freddy away from the Bible, from any books. Obey me in this."

"All right, Hugh," said his wife sadly. "I want to do the right thing. I will not teach Freddy any more."

"He'd better go to bed."

"Good night, Freddy." Sophia did not touch his cheek, as usual. Even little Tommy did not run for his customary good-night hug.

Frederick made his way up the narrow stairway slowly. *So,* he thought, *Mr. Hugh says that learning to read would ruin me as a slave forever. Then that is just what I am goin' to do. I am goin' to find some way to make myself the worst slave in the world.*

He climbed into his bed, but the warm covers did not comfort him as usual. For the first time since he came to Baltimore, Frederick felt once more like Old Master's Fed.

Frederick missed his reading lessons deeply. He ached when he saw Miss Sophia go into the parlor evenings with her Bible, knowing that he was not allowed to listen to the rich, poetic words of wisdom. But he would read for himself someday. Some way!

Frederick was very busy these days helping Miss Sophia care for the little ones. Ann Elizabeth started crawling early, and Frederick marveled at the efficiency with which she could find trouble.

"Let's go play outside, Freddy!" Tommy wanted his share of attention.

"Freddy will take you out to play when Ann Elizabeth takes her nap," said his mother, smiling wearily. She was already expecting another baby and felt drained and ill most of the time. Sophia touched Frederick's cheek. What would she do without him?

Frederick had tried to stay angry with his mistress, but her kindness and obvious exhaustion melted his antagonism away. It was Mr. Hugh's fault that he could not read, he decided, not Miss Sophia's. Frederick smiled at her.

Frederick helped feed Tommy and clean up. They went outside to throw a rag ball while Annie and her mother rested. When she called them in, Frederick was glad to note that Miss Sophia looked more like herself.

"Freddy," she said, "I need a paper of pins and a darning needle. Please go to Mr. Samuels's store and buy them for me. You may have this penny."

"*Thanks,* Miss Sophia!" This was extraordinary. Maybe Miss Sophia was sorry that his reading lessons had ended, too.

Where would he spend his penny? At Mistress Kelly's, where the fragrance of her luscious pastries tortured his nostrils every time he did errands? At Mr. Samuels's store, where he could get a stick of tangy horehound candy?

Frederick bought the sewing supplies at Mr. Samuels's, but decided that the aroma from Mrs. Kelly's was too good to resist. He selected a cinnamon bun and munched it ecstatically on the way home.

"What you doin', Lem?" asked Frederick as he passed a white boy a year or two older than he, scrawling on a fence. Frederick had discovered that most of the children in his neighborhood did not notice his color any more than they did their own. He had made several friends who fished with him occasionally.

"My brother and me, we keep track here of how many times we help my Uncle William on his boat," explained

Lem. "That way, when he gives us a sixpence, we know who should get what."

Frederick stared at the mysterious letters. "That's the letter b, I know," said Frederick. "What's that? Show me how to make it."

"Give me bite of your cinnamon bun first," said Lem, whose brother rarely got the best of a bargain with him.

A bite of cinnamon bun! Frederick hated to share his treat with the stingy Lem, but the lure of the unknown letters drew him. He held the bun out to Lem, who tried to grasp it.

"No, I will hold it," insisted Frederick. "You take your bite, then show me two letters. No, three."

Lem grinned at his fellow barterer. He took a large bite that made Frederick wince, then said gallantly, "I'll show you four. Looky here."

The two scrawled in the dirt with sticks, and Frederick learned the letters e, v, t, and p.

"Would you show me some more sometime?" asked Frederick.

"Any time—if you got cinnamon buns, that is."

"I don't," said Frederick, crestfallen. "I don't get them much." Then he brightened. "How about if I was to get you one of Miss Sophia's sweet biscuits?"

"I guess I would do it for one of them. Only two letters, though."

"I'll bring you one as soon as I can!" The two boys shook hands, and Frederick hurried home, downing the last of his cinnamon bun.

Hugh Auld seemed completely preoccupied with his business ventures. Frederick was glad that his master had shown even less interest in him since the disastrous reading exhibition.

Hugh seemed oblivious to everything but current prices for shipbuilding. He had not even heard the commotion in the streets last night that had awakened both Frederick and Miss Sophia.

A heavy, metallic clanking first interrupted the quiet. Frederick had listened drowsily, trying to decipher the sound. Was someone yanking at the latch of the house? But gradually he realized that he knew the sound all too well. It was the rattling of slave chains, heavy fetters clasped around the ankles of slaves headed for the slave market. Frederick covered his head with his pillow, but he still heard the ugly noise, then the bitter wails of women weeping. Austin Woolfolk, a prominent slave trader from Baltimore, often transported his slaves at night through the streets of the city to a holding pen behind his attractive middle-class home in a prosperous neighborhood. There they awaited their fate, usually a trip down South to the sugar cane and cotton fields. Woolfolk was an excellent businessman. Plantation owners who felt a little squeamish about separating spouses or selling children away from their families knew their slaves would be fed, treated well, and given adequate medical care while they were in Mr. Woolfolk's custody. He would see that they had proper homes. He also took care of confidential matters, such as the selling of a plantation owner's bastard children so that he would not have to constantly deal with his wife's wrath. Austin Woolfolk was indeed the picture of genteel discretion.

Frederick shivered, trying to shelter his soul from the hopeless keening of the women. Living with Hugh was far from ideal, but the nightmare of any slave was being sold down South. Would he himself some day make the trip to that unknown hell?

The next morning Frederick was bleary-eyed and

morose. He was quick to note that Miss Sophia looked as bad as he did.

"I heard Woolfolk coming through last night," she said.

Hugh grunted, buttering his hominy. "Wish they'd find some other route to his pen."

Miss Sophia's eyes filled with tears. "I can't bear it," she murmured. Black circles bruised the thin white skin under her eyes. She wilted under the growing burden of her child. Hugh put his arm around his wife in a rare show of tenderness.

"There, there, m'dear," he soothed, "I'll send Freddy for my sister Mercy. She'll come so you can get some rest. You are overwrought. Freddy, run as fast as you can to Mercy's. Tell her I'd be much obliged if she'd help us out."

Frederick grabbed his cap and flew out the door on his errand. *Miss Sophia won't teach me to read, but she don't like that Woolfolk either. I'm safe as long as I'm with her.*

Hugh's sister Mercy was as merry as he was taciturn. She arrived in a hurricane of clean blankets, hot soup, and friendly smiles. She was almost as big as her brother, and her energy seemed boundless. By the end of the day, the house and children were all scrubbed spotless, piles of cornbread filled the pantry, and a mountain of molasses cookies filled several stone jars. The next day, Miss Sophia played with her children and read from her Bible in the parlor while Mercy washed and ironed. Miss Sophia felt so rested that Mercy departed for her own home by supper time.

"Sing us a song, Freddy," said Miss Sophia as she tied a bib around Annie's plump little neck.

Frederick was glad to see some color in her cheeks. He sang a hymn she had taught him (Hugh had not forbidden their singing together), and the children tried to join in. It was a warm, happy household that greeted Hugh that evening.

Frederick was puzzled. Hugh was obviously happy to see his wife's improvement. He smiled into her eyes, jounced his daughter on his lap, and wrestled with Tommy until he squealed with delight. But Frederick knew his master well enough to know something was bothering him. Had the shipbuilding prices fallen again? Frederick took extra care in helping out, hoping his presence would not antagonize the man. When Hugh instructed him to head for bed not long after the little ones, Frederick complied readily. But he paused on the stairway, and heard Hugh speak to Miss Sophia.

"M' dear, I'm afraid I have some rather difficult news. Captain Anthony died a while back, and I just received the message today. The law says all his property has to be gathered down there and distributed to his heirs. That means we have to send Freddy back to Talbot County. He'll probably go to one of Captain Anthony's sons."

"Freddy? Go back? Oh, no, they can't take him! They might sell him South! Hugh, you must—"

"M' dear, I would do something if I could. But Freddy is the Anthony family's property, not ours. They were generous in loaning him to us this long."

Frederick stood like a statue on the stairs. Miss Sophia's weeping swirled around his ears like gray rain clouds. It sounded like that of Woolfolk's slave women.

four

Frederick, Miss Sophia, and Tommy made their way to Smith's Wharf, as they had so many times before for picnics and holidays. They passed Mrs. Kelly's pastry shop, and Miss Sophia impulsively bought Frederick and Tommy each a crusty, warm cinnamon bun, even though Frederick knew that the Aulds had little money these days. She herself was not hungry.

Frederick tried to enjoy it, but decided to keep his bun to eat on the boat. The last time he had traveled, Rich had seen that he ate, but the *Wildcat* was not the *Sally Lloyd;* he would probably know no one on this voyage.

"Look at the big frigate anchored over there!" Frederick marveled. She was a work of art, with large white sails that billowed in the chilly October breeze. "I—I wish that I could sail on her."

"I wish you could, too, dear," said Sophia Auld. "But here is the *Wildcat.*"

She spoke to the muscular black hand who was issuing orders to the others. Would they please make sure Frederick did not get too close to the rails? Did they have a place where he would keep warm?

Yes, yes, to all her questions. The man was polite, but he had to get this barge to the Eastern Shore on time.

"Boarding time, ma'am."

Sophia Auld threw her arms around Frederick, tears rolling down her cheeks and onto his head. Tommy clung to Frederick, alarmed at his mother's grief. Frederick felt as if his heart would explode.

"Take good care of him," choked Sophia, and suddenly Frederick was trying to wave a brave good-bye to the weeping woman and child on the shore.

"We almost there," said Rollo, the deckhand who had talked with Miss Sophia. "Finish yo' breakfast."

Rollo had treated Frederick decently, but this journey held no shining hope as his first to Baltimore had. Every mouthful of the tough, grainy cornbread caught in his throat and made him cough.

The barge anchored at a rude dock, and Rollo hallooed for someone to unload the cargo: a box of farm tools and Frederick. A slave from the distant primitive farmhouse responded, and Frederick followed the man to Holme Hill Farm, where he had been born.

"Oh, my baby come home!" shouted someone.

Frederick paused indignantly, but soon forgot his ire at being called a baby. For the old woman that raced to meet him was Grandmammy Bailey! Other familiar faces soon gathered: siblings Perry, now fifteen, Sarah and Eliza, as well as two other sisters he had never met: Kitty and Arianna. Frederick's plantation playmates, Nancy, Tom, Phil, and Jerry also appeared, along with Aunt Katy, who ignored him, much to Frederick's relief. Esther, beautiful as ever, nursed a baby. *Had she ever married Ned Roberts?* Frederick wondered. *Or is the child perhaps my half-brother, the son of Old Master?* He pushed the thought away.

"You are so growed," said his grandmother. "And so city-fine, too."

Frederick had forgotten how different his life in Baltimore was from life on the Eastern Shore. His relatives gaped at his jacket; clean, blue calico shirt tucked carefully into his knickers; warm, wooly socks that Miss Sophia had knit for him, and sturdy shoes.

"I'm almost ten," he told her. "Ten years old in February."

His brother and sisters giggled. "How he do talk," said Perry, grinning.

"More fancy than Old Master ever did."

"Hush yo' mouth, Perry," warned his grandmother. "You don't talk so about Old Master. We keep quiet till the Young Masters figger out where we go. We don't make no trouble."

Cemetery quiet, like that in the Lloyds' graveyard, descended on the group. But Frederick had to know. "Can I go with Miss Lucretia?" Miss Lucretia was not Miss Sophia, but she had been kind to him, and during the lonely hours Frederick floated away from all he loved in Baltimore, he cherished the hope that Miss Lucretia would rescue him.

"Fed," said Grandmammy gently, "None of us knows where we go. We will all go with Miss Lucretia and her husban', Captain Auld, or Young Masters Andrew or Richard. We jus' wait till we hear."

Tears of rage welled up in Frederick's eyes. He buried his wet face in Grandmammy's comforting bosom, sniffling angrily, and she held him as if he were four again.

"Where is that boy!" shouted Andrew Anthony.

Frederick shrank back into the corner of the cold kitchen, where he had spent a restless night. How he missed his cozy straw mattress!

Master Andrew swung at the air in a familiar movement that made Frederick shiver; it was too much like Old Master's. Master Andrew reeked of liquor.

"Where is he?" he screamed. "I need him to get my horse ready to hunt!"

Grandmammy tried to answer calmly, but even her serene voice trembled. "Let us find 'im for you, sir, if you tell us who you lookin' for."

Andrew Anthony swore at the old woman and raged out to the creek, where the young slaves often fished before dawn.

"Fed!" cried his grandmother. "Hurry down to the creek and tell 'em Young Master Andrew's comin'. Run!"

Frederick tore out of the back of the cabin, trying to make his way as quietly and rapidly as possible through the woods. He could see Perry several hundred yards away, intent on the trout he had been trying to catch for several days. He did not hear Andrew charging through the brush behind him!

The demented man struck the boy with a stunning blow that knocked him flat. He grabbed Perry by the throat and slammed him into a tree trunk, throwing him to the ground, then grinding his boot heel into his head. Perry lay motionless, warm blood dribbling from his mouth and ears.

Frederick had not realized he was standing in the open, screaming. Andrew Anthony glared at him, kicked Perry one more time, and said menacingly, "*That* is the way I will serve you, one of these days."

He turned and disappeared like an evil spirit.

"Thirsty, Perry?"

Frederick handed his brother the gourdful of water;

Perry tried to smile, but his lips were still blue and swollen, and there was a gap where he had lost teeth. He improved daily in body and spirit. But Frederick alternated between brooding anger and paralyzing fear; his nights were full of phantoms that stalked him, rattling their chains.

"What if we go to Master Andrew, Perry?"

"Figger we do the best we can."

"What if he sells us down South?" The slaves had already surmised that Andrew's heavy drinking and gambling would quickly diminish his inheritance. If Andrew needed cash—what better way to raise quick money than to sell a few slaves?

"Fed," Perry said, "y'all think too much. Always did. Mebbe we go to Andrew. Mebbe we be sold down South. Mebbe not. But worryin' ain't gonna help you or me either one. So we wait, and mebbe things get better."

Frederick shook his head; the overseer's wake-up horn sounded, and he left to harvest the turnips and sweet potatoes that still grew in the huge garden. He hated the dirt, the chilly autumn mornings, the very smell of knobby root vegetables. But work made time pass.

One day, however, there was no overseer's horn. The twenty-nine slaves that had belonged to Old Master gathered before a district official and James Chambers and William Leonard, both longtime friends of Old Master. Together they decreed the distribution. Grandmammy and Frederick's siblings went to Andrew Anthony, along with his Aunt Betty and her two small children. They were to stay at Holme Hill Farm, which was also part of Andrew's share of the estate. Aunt Katy, her two youngest children, and her man Harry were decreed to Richard Anthony. Thomas and Lucretia Auld received Frederick's Aunt Milly, her four children, and Frederick himself!

47

The executors continued their work, but Frederick did not hear any more. He breathed a sigh of relief that went clear down to his toes.

But when the entire distribution was finished, and Captain Auld and Miss Lucretia signaled Frederick and their other slaves to follow them home, Frederick paused. Grandmammy stood, straight and tall, as usual, with her arms around the girls, who cuddled little Harriet. Perry hobbled to her side. Their eyes were blank, empty. When Andrew Anthony nodded curtly, they followed in a slow, sad parade. Frederick stared after them as long as he could. Would he ever see his grandmammy, his brother, and sisters again?

"Fed, I need to speak with you."

Frederick stopped scrubbing the floor and stood before Miss Lucretia. He was not fond of kitchen chores, but without Aunt Katy, Old Master's kitchen had brightened considerably.

"Captain Auld and I feel it would be best if you returned to Baltimore to help Mr. Hugh's family."

Frederick's jaw dropped in amazement.

Miss Lucretia laughed and patted him on the head. "You will depart tomorrow, that is, if you finish all your work today." She left chuckling mischievously as Frederick attacked the floor as if it were an enemy.

Back to Baltimore! Back to Miss Sophia and Tommy, back to his own room with a warm bed, back to the wharves and sailing ships and fried chicken on Sundays! Frederick could hardly keep from turning a flip, a new skill he had learned from Perry. But he had plenty to do, so he sang at the top of his lungs as he worked: "O Canaan, sweet Canaan, I am goin' to that blessed, sweet land of Canaan!"

Miss Lucretia, hemming tea towels in the parlor, smiled.

"Boy, you like a jumpin' jack!" grinned Rich. "Quit that poppin' up and down! You cain't sit still for a minute!"

"Will we be there soon, Rich?"

" 'Bout an hour, if you don't sink the boat first."

Finally the sloop pulled into Smith's Wharf. Miss Sophia waved her handkerchief frantically, and Tommy clapped his hands. Frederick leaped from the boat, and the three hugged joyously.

"Oh, Freddy, we didn't know you'd come back to us!" Miss Sophia looked drawn and thin, despite her protruding middle. Frederick resolved to help her as much as possible. He put Tommy on his shoulders as they headed home.

The next year was a busy one for the Auld family and Frederick. Hugh fulfilled a lifelong dream by forming his shipbuilding partnership. Miss Sophia gave birth to Benjamin, and the growing family moved to a house on Philpot Street that was closer to Hugh's business.

Frederick had hoped Hugh would forget his opposition to his education. One afternoon when the babies and Miss Sophia were napping, he slipped a treasure from its hiding place behind the pantry cupboard. It was a scrap of newspaper that he had rescued from the street. Frederick pored over it, trying to find all the a's and b's and other letters he knew. Somehow, it was trying to tell him something, and he could not decipher what it was.

"Freddy!"

Frederick started guiltily. Miss Sophia threw the newspaper into the fireplace.

"Freddy, your master works very hard to take care of us all. If it is his wish that you refrain from reading, then we must respect that. Do not bring such a thing into this house again." Sophia Auld grasped Frederick's thin shoulders and stared into his frightened eyes. "Now go chop some more wood."

Why won't Miss Sophia help me read? Is she afraid of Mr. Hugh?

Frederick flailed away at the dry logs, glad to vent his anger and confusion. *But I am going to read,* he resolved. *Miss Sophia may take away my newspapers, and Mr. Hugh may think I've forgotten about it, but I am going to read.*

Hugh decided that Frederick would be useful at his shipyard. Frederick loved watching the carpenters plane and hammer the clean, fragrant wood. He observed their marking lumber with chalk to indicate its destination: "s" for starboard, "l" for larboard, "sa" for starboard aft, and "sf" for starboard forward. While all of the workers ate their noonday meals, Frederick slipped into the main room and practiced drawing the letters in the sawdust with a stick.

He also devised a way to get free tutoring from neighborhood boys. Frederick would practice his letters on a fence two or three blocks away from the Auld house. Inevitably, another boy stopped to watch him.

"Beat that if you can," Frederick challenged him, having drawn the best s or f that he could.

"That? That ain't nothin'!" and his "teacher" would draw a whole row of g's, h's, i's, and j's. "How old are ya? Eleven? And you can't read?"

"No, but I'm gonna." Frederick immediately began to practice the new letters.

Frederick gained friends, as well as teachers, through this trick. They were the sons of white shipbuilders, but they pitched pennies with Frederick, played ball with him, and welcomed his help fighting any other boys who dared cross into their territory. Frederick was formidable in the battles they shared, and he earned their respect quickly.

Tommy progressed rapidly in school, and his proud parents carefully kept all his copybooks and a Webster spelling book in the parlor cupboard. Frederick could not keep away from the great wealth of knowledge stored there. He stealthily practiced the alphabet between the lines of the copybooks and studied the speller until he could write the words on scrap pine boards that he "borrowed" from the lumberyard and hid in his room.

But he remembered the grand words of the Bible that Miss Sophia read, and longed to hear them again.

"All men must repent before God," declared Rev. Hanson, a white Methodist minister who occasionally preached at Sophia Auld's church. "All are sinners, whether free or in bonds, great or small. All can and must come to God through Jesus Christ." Thirteen-year-old Frederick drank in the amazing words.

I am a sinner, he admitted to himself. *That I know is true. I hate the white people who hurt my family. I want to hurt them. I hate Woolfolk and his slave marches at night. I don't know God. I don't understand Him. What can I do?*

Frederick wrestled with his conscience for weeks. He finally talked with a lay preacher, Charles Johnson, from the Bethel African Methodist Church, who told him to seek God and pray. Frederick did, as he carried firewood, fetched water, and took messages to Hugh's customers.

God, do you really love black people?

Why do we suffer so?

How can You love white people that hurt others?

Do You really love me? Did You die for me, too?

I don't have a father. Are you my Father, as well as Miss Sophia's and Tommy's?

One Sunday morning Frederick was in the back pew of Bethel Church. He felt like a moth attracted to a brilliant flame—his mind and heart full of pain, but pulled irresistibly toward the light.

Rev. Nathaniel Peck's thunderous sermon only agitated him further. God was holy. God would punish sinners. Frederick's stomach churned.

"Do you love the Lord, son?" asked an older man sitting near him.

"I—I want to," answered Frederick.

The man laughed gently, his dark face shining with joy. "What your name?"

"Frederick," answered the boy.

"Well, Frederick, all God ask is that we want to love Him. He knows none of us can't do it without His help. Do you believe the Lord Jesus die for your sins?"

"Yes, sir."

"And that God want to love you forever?"

"Yes, sir." And suddenly, Frederick did! Later he wrote, "I finally found that change of heart which comes by 'casting all one's care' upon God, and by having faith in Jesus Christ, as the Redeemer, Friend, and Savior of those who diligently seek Him."[1] The weeks of tortuous self-examination and despair were over. "After this, I saw the world in a new light. I seemed to live in a new world, surrounded by new objects, and to be animated by new hopes and desires. I loved all mankind—slaveholders not excepted; though I abhorred slavery more than ever. My great concern was now to have the world converted."[2]

Frederick eagerly joined the Bethel African Methodist Church. Every Sunday morning the boy rose early to complete his chores so he could sit by Charles Lawson, the elderly freedman who had reassured him of his salvation.

He soon became "Uncle Lawson" to the lonely child who craved a father's guidance. They were a poignant, yet amusing sight to the congregation—the lanky, long-legged boy and the bent, grizzled old man. Frederick loved the hours he spent praying, singing, and reading the Bible aloud at Uncle Lawson's little shack on Sundays. Hugh growled at such a waste of time, and even threatened to whip Frederick, but Sophia defended him. He continued to enjoy rapid spiritual and educational growth as Uncle Lawson encouraged him.

"The Lord has a great work for you to do," said Uncle Lawson.

"A great work?" Frederick's serious brown eyes lit up. "But I am a slave for life. How can these things be—and what can I do?" His young shoulders slumped. His hands tightened into fists.

"Trust in the Lord," said Uncle Lawson. "The Lord can make you free, my dear. All things are possible with Him, only *have faith in God*."[3] The man's mild voice suddenly became commanding. "We will pray about this, Frederick." So, for the first time, Frederick began to ask God to deliver him from slavery.

Uncle Lawson prayed constantly as he drove wagons all over Baltimore. Frederick soon surpassed his teacher in pronouncing the hard words in the worn Bible that Uncle Lawson gave him, but the old man was a model of godliness and prayer throughout Frederick's life.

If I have any chance under heaven of being free, Frederick thought, *it'll be a bigger one because of Uncle Lawson's prayers.*

five

I t's them abolitionists," said Hugh sourly.

"Causin' all the trouble," agreed his assistant. "I'm glad they gave Nat Turner what he deserved, but he got them abolitionists all stirred up."

It was not the first time Frederick had heard conversations like this. New words intrigued him, but this one seemed to cause explosions whenever he heard it. He managed to look up "abolition" in the Aulds' dictionary, but it only defined the word as "the act of abolishing."

Abolishing what? What would cause such dark looks, such oaths? Frederick detected fear, as well as rage in their reactions. He had to find out.

One day he read a news article in the *Baltimore American,* a newspaper that printed editorials from abolitionist publications, then tried to respond with answers that supported the slavery system. John Quincy Adams, the paper stated, brought to Congress petitions from Pennsylvania Quakers, who declared that slavery was a terrible evil and wanted it abolished in the nation's capital.

Slavery in Washington, D.C., was an affront to God, said the abolitionists.

They believe slavery is wrong, thought Frederick. *There are white people who believe slavery is wrong.*

He breathlessly read the rest of the story. Congress did not support the statement, of course. John Quincy Adams himself did not support it. But from what Frederick could tell, there were a large number of people in the North who believed slavery was wrong.

Frederick sat motionless.

The world he knew suddenly tipped crazily, wonderfully. He felt as if gravity could not hold his feet on the ground.

No wonder the Marylanders were so afraid. No wonder they carefully censored all news from the North, forbade their slaves to read, discouraged their contact with freedmen.

Frederick continued to collect newspaper scraps whenever he could, hiding them under his mattress. Soon he discovered that there were free states and slave states. Free states. That must mean that there were entire geographical areas in which no one could own slaves.

He had not known.

Why had they not told him?

There it is. I'm going to buy it!

Frederick's friends loathed the essays from the *Columbian Orator* that they had to memorize at school. But when his friend George practiced his speech by the Roman, Cato, the lines on liberty caught Frederick's attention. He was determined to read it himself. He took his cherished fifty cents, which he had earned shining boots, to Mr. Nathaniel Knight's bookstore.

The storekeeper had no idea why Mr. Auld's Negro

wanted to purchase a book of oratory.

"It's for Tommy, as soon as he gets bigger," said Frederick.

Mr. Knight sold him the secondhand copy. Frederick hid the book in his jacket and hurried home so that he might savor his treasure in his attic room. He had painstakingly worked his way through the Bible, a Methodist hymnal, and many fragments of newspapers and pamphlets. Now a whole new world spoke to him in the weighty, difficult works of Cato, Washington, Socrates, and others that praised the virtues of liberty, democracy, self-control, and hard work. "Dialogue Between a Master and Slave," by the abolitionist editor Caleb Bingham, changed Frederick's thinking forever. In it a recaptured runaway slave was reproached by his master for his actions. The slave answered his master so well that the master freed him. Needless to say, the Aulds would not have approved of his reading material! Frederick re-read the essay.

Why should Mr. Hugh and Miss Sophia deserve my gratitude? thought Frederick. *They have been kind to me, but mostly for their own purposes, much as they are kind to animals. They have stolen my freedom from me, as a robber steals money. Surely God has not ordained my slavery, any more than He would ordain a thief's making off with Mr. Hugh's payroll.*

"Freddy," said Sophia Auld sharply. "You are not listening to me. You must clean out the fireplace today and churn for me."

Frederick stared at her sullenly. He much preferred working in the shipyard to kitchen chores.

"What is the matter with you?" said Sophia angrily. "You used to be so pleasant, so helpful." The moody teenager that glared at her in no way resembled the eager child who had readily served as her right-hand man. "I shall tell your master if you do not cooperate. Now, get to it before I take a switch to you myself!"

Still silent, Frederick began to sweep the ashes.

Sophia rubbed her pounding temples. She had had another baby, little Hugh, only months before, and was still weak and tired. Hugh's business ventures were not going well, and he drank excessively. Frederick was rarely at home, except on Saturdays; with four children and a household to tend, she needed his help! What possessed him to be so difficult? Sophia had no experience with teenagers; she did not realize Frederick's behavior was normal.

Frederick performed adequately, but did not jump to help his mistress as he had before. She was becoming shrewish, he decided; slavery had taken its toll on her kind nature. It did not occur to him until much later that Sophia might find it impossible to deal with his obstinate attitude.

Even Tommy had absorbed the attitudes of his peers; Frederick was no longer his best friend. He was his servant.

With tension between him and those he loved, Frederick decided to keep as much distance between him and Hugh as possible. But his new demeanor did not pass unnoticed.

"If that slave wasn't so much help, I'd send him back to Thomas tomorrow," declared Hugh. "We need to keep an eye on him."

"He *is* a great deal of help," Sophia said quickly. She fought with Frederick, but Sophia still loved him. *I must not give Hugh the impression I want Freddy to go.* Besides, she was not sure how she would make it without him, especially now Henny was here. Sophia sighed.

Several months before, Thomas Auld had sent his brother another slave, Frederick's cousin Henny. But

Henny's hands were scarred, curled uselessly from falling into a fire as a small child. Although she could carry heavy loads, she was of little help to Sophia, and presented another mouth to feed. Hugh had little patience with the slow-thinking Henny; one day when her load of firewood slipped and nearly fell on the baby, Hugh made up his mind. Brother Thomas had indeed been generous in loaning Frederick to them, but Hugh did have to feed and board him, as well as tolerate his presence. And Hugh certainly was under no obligation to receive every useless slave Thomas owned. He unceremoniously sent Henny back to Talbot County.

Thomas exploded. So this was the thanks he received for his charity? He immediately sent word that Frederick was also to return to his home in St. Michaels.

Sophia wept; Frederick had lived with them five years. Hugh raged helplessly. But the law was the law. Thomas owned Frederick, and to St. Michaels he would go.

I wish Jesus had come the other night, thought Frederick. He and hundreds of other Christians had greeted a spectacular meteor shower as a sign of the Second Coming only weeks before. Frederick had strained his eyes, looking for his Savior who would rescue him from the misery of leaving Baltimore. But Jesus had not come, and now Frederick rode through the March gloom on the sloop *Amanda.* His only consolation was watching the steamers make their ponderous way toward Philadelphia. Philadelphia was in a free state—Pennsylvania, he knew. *One day I'll take a boat to Philadelphia,* he thought. *I'll run away.*

As the *Amanda* approached St. Michaels, Frederick grew more despondent. He had long contemplated an escape plan in Baltimore, where there were thousands of free blacks, many modes of transportation, and numerous hiding places. But St. Michaels was located on a long, thin peninsula; it would be difficult to leave it without being noticed. As the sloop docked, Frederick noted the unpainted shacks that were home to the population of uneducated oystermen. St. Michaels boasted a fine brick house or two and a few primitive stores, but the vast majority of the town was dirty and disgusting, Frederick decided.

The next few weeks did nothing to improve his opinion of the place. Frederick easily discerned that the majority of the white population was less educated than he was. He despised their straw hats, bare feet, and ignorant rural ways. They, in turn, were immediately suspicious of the tall black man who looked them boldly in the eye and walked around town in his city clothes with his nose in the air.

Frederick hated his new mistress, a demanding, rude woman whose health was already deteriorating with "consumption," or tuberculosis. Rowena Auld, whom Thomas had married after Miss Lucretia's death, also mistreated her stepdaughter, a meek seven-year-old with her mother's mild blue eyes. Frederick shook with fury when Rowena struck the child. She also allowed her slaves only a half-peck of cornmeal a week, half of what a slave on Colonel Lloyd's plantation was given. Rowena locked the food away and kept the key with her at all times. She'd rather let meat spoil, she told the kitchen slaves, than let lazy slaves eat it up.

To fifteen-year-old Frederick, who increased in height almost daily, this was unforgivable. No matter how much he clashed with Hugh and Sophia, they always made sure Frederick had plenty to fill up his long, hollow legs. Now he could hardly sleep at night because of hunger.

Frederick had resented Hugh, but he loathed Thomas. "When I lived with Captain Auld, I thought him incapable of a noble action. His leading characteristic was intense self-ishness. I think he was himself fully aware of this fact and often tried to conceal it. . . . There was in him all the love of domination, the pride of mastery, and the swagger of authority, but his rule lacked the vital element of consistency."[1]

The only bright spot in his new existence was his seventeen-year-old sister Eliza; they lived with Henny and their Aunt Priscilla in the Aulds' kitchen. Eliza knew her brother was headed for imminent disaster.

"You got to learn to act like a slave, Fed," she urged, "or you gonna be sold down South for sure." Eliza had already informed Frederick that Andrew Anthony had drunk himself further into debt, and sold their sister Sarah, their Aunt Betty, and her children to a man from Mississippi the year before, just as the Bailey slaves had feared. Andrew died soon afterwards.

"We ain't heard what they gonna do with Grand-mammy and the others," Eliza told him. "They sent me here. But times is bad, and Master Thomas just might decide to get some easy money from selling you if you don't behave."

Frederick shivered. Did life just keep spiraling down into deeper, darker evil?

"I'm gonna run away," he told Eliza.

"Keep yo' mouth shut!" she spat. "This ain't Baltimore. Right now you gotta think about keepin' alive. You won't be for long, if you ever say that again! Peter and me, he work day and night, I save my pennies till he can buy me and the girls. That how I gonna get away from Miss Rowena. It take two years, maybe three, but we gonna do it. *You,* Mr. High-and-Mighty, you better make a plan, and it better be some-thin' smarter than openin' your big mouth!"

Frederick knew Eliza was right. He had seen her brush

Rowena's long hair by the hour to be rewarded with a couple of coppers. Eliza also wove beautiful baskets that she sold in Thomas's store; she pocketed only a small fraction of the profits, while Thomas took the rest. But her tiny pile of money hoarded behind a brick in the fireplace slowly grew, and with it her dreams of marriage to a freedman named Peter Mitchell, who had fathered her two little girls.

"You're right," Frederick admitted humbly. "What do I do?"

"Fust, you gotta stop lookin' white people in the face! Smile and say, 'yassir,' and 'no'm', and 'yo' sholy is right, Mas'r'! Take food whenever you kin, 'cause you ain't gonna get none here."

"Isn't that stealing?" Frederick could not reconcile such actions with his still-fervent Christian beliefs.

"*They* steal food from my babies," said Eliza. "I only take what I can find to keep us alive. They think we're animals," Eliza said, "so they're not surprised if we act like animals. What upsets them is when we act like human beings."

Frederick learned to slip a biscuit into his sleeve when he served the Aulds breakfast. He drank water in which meat had been boiled and pilfered fresh peas and beans from the garden. *After all,* he thought, *the food and I are both property, Captain Auld's property. The food does not really change hands; it is simply relocated. And it benefits his property.* When he took food outside of the Auld household, Frederick regarded it as lately paid wages for the slavery that society perpetuated.

Eliza taught Frederick to work slowly and rest when his supervisors were absent. "Why work yo'self to death?" she demanded. "You ain't never goin' to finish yo' work, and y'all don't get paid none."

Eliza also told Frederick that their mistress disliked their calling her husband "Captain Auld," which she regarded as too informal. "Call him 'Master,' " Rowena had insisted angrily. The two teenagers simply "disremembered" this instruction and continued to address Thomas as "Captain Auld."

Frederick, too, "disremembered" to tie up Captain Auld's horse, which always bolted for Rowena's father's farm, where it had been raised. Infuriated, Thomas usually ordered Frederick to walk to the Hambleton plantation, where Aunt Mary, a cook who deplored Frederick's skinny state, loaded him with baked goods. Frederick then rode home and shared his booty with Eliza and the others.

"Fed," Captain Auld said one morning, "Mrs. Auld and I are going to camp meeting tomorrow. You will accompany us."

Frederick was pleased, though not elated. A change— any change—from life at the Aulds had to be a change for the better. He occasionally went to a small black Sabbath school with freedmen, but knew he had learned far more from Uncle Lawson than any of them knew. He was not permitted to teach because of his slave status. Perhaps at camp meeting he would hear Scriptural teaching that would help him grow to love God more. He was curious, too, about his master's spiritual state. Thomas Auld was unusual in that he had little to do with the area churches. Why was he going to camp meeting?

Camp meeting was not Baltimore, Frederick told himself, but it was certainly exciting. Hundreds of carriages and wagons rolled in; rows of tents sprang up. Boatloads of salvation-seekers arrived by river. All came to hear the nonstop preaching from a large platform in the middle of a campground. Slaves like Frederick chopped wood to feed the huge communal fire where oxen and hogs were roasted along with sweet potatoes and sugar corn to feed the huge crowds.

One day, as Frederick and other blacks stood in the small section reserved for them behind the speaker, he spotted his master making his way forward to a mourner's area, a fenced-in, straw-covered section in front of the speaker where whites could repent of their sins and pray. Blacks, of course, were not allowed in front of the preacher. Frederick was surrounded by his fellow slaves shouting "hallelujah," dancing, and falling to the ground in religious ecstasy, as many of the white people did. Frederick edged as close to the white area as he dared. Would Captain Thomas Auld "come through"? Would he be changed from the cruel man who denied his slaves food and beat Henny mercilessly because he wanted her to die and thus rid himself of the inconvenience? Would the love of Christ even help him understand that he should love his slaves enough to give them the freedom that he himself cherished? Frederick watched Thomas Auld utter a groan; one tear trickled slowly down his cheek. Compared to the emotional tumult around him, Captain Auld's conversion experience seemed sparse, at best.

We'll see when we get back, thought Frederick.

Thomas Auld did indeed change when he returned to St. Michaels. His house suddenly became a headquarters for Methodist circuit riders, most of whom seemed far more concerned with the chicken and dumplings and sweet potato pie in front of them than the eternal destinies of the hungry slaves serving them.

Prayer meetings continued day and night in the Auld home. Rev. George Cookman, an Englishman who had left a profitable business to become a minister, was the only one to invite Thomas Auld's slaves to attend the meetings. He often asked the slaves penetrating questions about their spiritual and physical welfare. Frederick and the others knew better than to answer honestly in front of the Aulds, but they sensed the concern Rev. Cookman had for them. Indeed, he tried to convince Methodists in the area, including Thomas Auld, to free their slaves—unsuccessfully.

Although the Methodist Discipline declared that no member who owned slaves should attain to an office in the church, Captain Auld was admitted to church membership (skipping the usual probationary period) and almost immediately began teaching and assisting at area revivals. Everyone was sure his conversion was genuine.

Except his slaves.

If anything, he became more harsh in his treatment of them.

Frederick, Eliza, and the others still were allowed only one-half peck of cornmeal per week. The pantry remained tightly locked.

Often displeased with Henny, Captain Auld would tie her up, whip her, leave her dangling from the ceiling joists for hours, return to eat dinner, and whip her again, quoting Luke 12:47: "That servant, which knew his lord's will, and prepared not himself, neither did according to his will, shall be beaten with many stripes."

Not surprised, but still deeply depressed by Auld and his church, Frederick was at an all-time spiritual low when a young white man named Wilson stopped him one day on the street.

"Fed, I hear that you are a student of the Scriptures," said Wilson.

"Yassir, Mr. Wilson," answered Frederick, "I love my Lord Jesus."

"So do I," said Wilson with a quiet elation that held

Frederick's heart. "And I know of many young Negroes who also cherish Him, but are unable to read the Holy Scriptures for themselves. Would you be willing, Fed, to help these lambs know more about the Savior?"

"I would love it more than anything!" said Frederick. He had begun to teach other blacks in Baltimore how to read the Bible, and missed the spiritual fellowship and intellectual stimulation that he had so enjoyed there.

"I felt I could count on you," said Wilson. "I have some old spellers and a few New Testaments. Do you think you could come to James Mitchell's home on Tuesday evening?"

"I'll do my best, Mr. Wilson," said Frederick fervently.

Tuesday Frederick worked with an industry and quickness that made Eliza shake her head at him. *Slow down,* he told himself. *Don't want to make them think something's up!*

"Want to go fishin', Fed?" asked Thomas with a knowing smile.

Frederick's heart fell into his feet. "M—Maybe," he answered.

Thomas was in a rare good mood. "Well, go, then. Trout would taste good."

Frederick took his fishing pole, a bag with his Bible and speller in it, and left before Auld could change his mind.

He took the back way to Mitchell's hut in the woods. When he tapped on the door, the freedman answered with a smile.

"Glad to see you, Fed!"

Twenty adults and children eyed Frederick as he opened his books. "First, we are going to ask for God's help in learning to read His Book," announced Mr. Wilson. "Then we are all going to learn the letters a, b, and c."

The pupils bowed their heads reverently for the blessing and then fastened their eyes hungrily on the letters Wilson and Frederick drew for them on rough pieces of pine board.

"A-b, ab," they chorused.

Frederick felt joy like a river flowing through his veins. . . .

"Fed, they don't like it." James Mitchell's heavy grizzled eyebrows met in the center of his forehead.

"Who don't like what?"

"Well, Mr. West, for one. He says our school's against the law."

"I thought Mr. Wilson said there is no law in Maryland that says Negroes can't be taught to read."

"Well, mebbe there ain't. But Mr. West and the white people in St. Michaels, they don't like our school."

Frederick felt his throat tighten. "What did Mr. Wilson say?"

"He say because it ain't against the law, he gonna teach the school."

"Then I'm gonna, too. Is it still at your house, James?"

"Them chilluns need to know about Jesus," he declared. "And we aydults, we need to know about Him, too. I be proud to have us learn to read the Holy Book in my house."

"Where you goin', Fed?"

"To catch us a trout or two, Captain Auld." Frederick waved his fishing pole.

"Hope you have better luck than last time," said Thomas.

Frederick felt Auld's penetrating eyes on him. Because Wilson had been accosted by angry whites as news of the black school had leaked out, he had decided to hold the school on different days each week. Frederick also went first to his fishing hole for an hour in case anyone followed him.

Please, God, he prayed as he threw in his line, *tell your fish to cooperate so that I can show some to Captain Auld when I get home.*

God's trout were evidently more obedient than some of His people, Frederick decided. He had an excellent hour of fishing. Then he slipped quietly through the woods to James's house.

Even more students awaited him this week.

"Look, Fed! There's a d and an a!" Simon, a shriveled field hand, pointed to Genesis 1:5. "What does the Bible say, Fed?"

"That word is 'Day,' " Frederick answered. "It says, 'God called the light Day.' "

"I read the Bible, Fed!" The elderly man looked at him in wonder. "I done read a word from God's Holy Book." He sat quietly for a moment. "Show me another one!"

But Frederick had no chance to help Simon. The door burst open. Garretson West pushed his huge bulk through it. Some in the community regarded the oysterman as a saint. He was illiterate, yet somehow the Spirit, according to his supporters, gave him wisdom from above. But there was nothing saintlike now in the expression in his small eyes.

"What you doin' here?"

"Sir, they are learning to read the Holy Scriptures." Wilson stepped forward, his face white, but set.

"I'll learn you to mess with the property of God-fearin' men!" West shoved the smaller man out the door and waved his club menacingly. Wrightson Fairbank, another "exhorter" from West's church, slammed James Mitchell against the wall.

"Git out o' here, all o' ya! Never come back!"

Frederick and the others scattered like leaves before a winter gale. But he saw Constable Thomas Graham, the

67

Aulds' next door neighbor, smashing the pine boards with their crude letters, ripping the spellers and New Testaments to shreds. Assisting him in his task was Thomas Auld himself.

West, Fairbank, Graham, Auld—they were all leaders in their church.

Frederick ran mechanically through blackberry brambles, his legs unfeeling as metal pistons. The whipping he would undoubtedly receive made no imprint on his mind.

They don't want Negroes to read the Bible.

They don't want Negroes to learn to love God's Son.

They don't want us to go to heaven.

Frederick felt cold, glowing rage spread inside him like a disease.

"Fed."

Frederick slowly put down his pail of water and ambled across the stable. He stared straight into Thomas's eyes, unblinking. The man winced. He thought his decision not to whip the boy for his part in the black school might make him grateful and more cooperative. Instead, Frederick went about his tasks as if in slow motion. The dark eyes always held a scornful smile.

"Fed, I've decided to rent you out to William Covey come the new year."

Frederick said nothing.

"Mr. Covey is a Christian man, and will teach you your duty to your betters."

Silence. Only the eyes.

"Back to work, Fed! I expect this stable to be clean, not like last week."

Frederick sauntered back.

Thomas Auld gritted his teeth. New Year's Day could not come too soon.

six

The bitter wind played with Frederick as if he were a toy. The ocean sometimes cheered him, its wild, uninhibited waves surging like the feelings inside him. But today, New Year's Day 1834, the Chesapeake Bay's somber gray depths only increased his misgivings as he made his way along Bayside Peninsula. Soon he would arrive at William Covey's farm.

Covey, he had heard from other slaves, was a "niggerbreaker," a man who made it his business to crush the spirits of rebellious slaves. Frederick shivered. He had heard frightening rumors about his new master. One bright possibility pierced the darkness like a candle: Covey worked you to death, but he fed you good. Frederick's empty stomach warmed at the thought.

Finally, Frederick spied a small house on the shores of the Bay; it looked as cheerless as its surroundings. But his outgrown Baltimore clothes did nothing to blunt the freezing knife of forty-mile-per-hour winds. He went to the back door and knocked.

A large, young black woman answered.

"Captain Auld sent me to work for Mr. Covey," Frederick said.

"Set over by the fire, and I get you somethin' to eat. Then I tell 'im you here."

Frederick savored the bowl of hot chowder; it was not Miss Sophia's chowder, of course, but there was lots of it, and the soup warmed his freezing bones like a magic potion. Perhaps it would not be too bad here, after all.

I'll kill him. Then I'll kill myself.

Frederick tried to screen himself from the bright sunshine that poured from a peaceful Sunday sky. Every joint in his body groaned in pain and exhaustion. His rough shirt clung to new, blood-encrusted welts on his back. Food was plentiful on Sundays, but Frederick could not summon enough energy to make his way to the back door.

Maybe I'll die sooner if I don't eat.

Frederick had ceased to care about eating, about reading, about anything. His soul-draining days often stretched from predawn hours to midnight during planting. "Mr. Covey succeeded in breaking me. I was broken in body, soul, and spirit," wrote Frederick much later. "My natural elasticity was crushed; my intellect languished; the disposition to read departed; the cheerful spark that lingered about my eye died; the dark night of slavery closed in upon me; and behold a man transformed into a brute!"[1]

On Frederick's second day at the Covey farm, his new master had ripped his clothes from him and whipped him savagely because the oxen Frederick drove broke a gate. Covey beat his new slave with barbaric regularity, as Frederick had few farm skills and was often awkward and slow in accomplishing the many tasks that had to be done.

70

Worst of all, Covey seemed obsessed with the idea that his slaves were lazy. *He binds heavy burdens, grievous to be borne, and lays them on men's shoulders, but will not move them with one of his fingers,* thought Frederick. Covey often hid behind fences, in thickets and cornfields, springing out to whip any slave who dared stop working for a moment. His workers secretly referred to him as "the Snake" because of his slyness and reptilian quickness. He would even leave on horseback as if he were going to St. Michaels, then sneak back, tie the horse in the woods, and observe his slaves' activities from ditches near the fields.

The Snake, however, became harmless as a dove on Sundays. His slaves did only minimal work while he and his family attended services. Covey provided a large dinner for them, and even postponed whippings until Monday morning. On Sunday evenings, Covey gathered his family and workers together to sing hymns. He often requested that Frederick lead them with his fine voice, but did not seem to take offense if he refused.

Covey's near-angelic Sundays did nothing to mend the evil of the rest of his week, thought Frederick.

He watched the glory of the white-sailed ships on the Bay, longing for their freedom. *You are loosed from your moorings, and free; I am fast in my chains, and am a slave! . . .O God, save me! God, deliver me! Let me be free! Is there any God?*[2]

Watching the ships eventually resurrected Frederick's near-dead dreams of escape. *Only think of it; one hundred miles straight north, and I am free! Try it? Yes! God helping me, I will. It cannot be that I shall live and die a slave. I will take to the water. . . . It may be that my misery in slavery will only increase my happiness when I get free. There is a better day coming.*[3]

71

The weary teenager drifted into a tormented sleep.

The sweltering July sun shone mercilessly as Covey's slaves hurried to harvest his wheat before the distant thunderheads erupted. Frederick, Bill, another rented slave, William Hughes, Covey's cousin, and Covey himself reaped, hauled, and threshed the crop as quickly as they could. Covey had promised that he would release his workers an hour before sunset if they finished by then. Frederick and the others looked forward to an evening fishing trip.

"Fed! Are you all right, Fed?"

Bill watched Frederick sway with dizziness, shake, then fall flat on his back.

"He got sunstroked, Mr. Covey! Look at 'im!"

Exhausted himself and frustrated by the delay, Covey kicked Frederick viciously in the side, then hit him with a heavy piece of hickory wood.

Frederick gradually returned to consciousness, but did not move until Covey went to the barn. Then he crawled slowly to a patch of shade next to a fence. Frederick forced himself to his feet and headed dizzily for the woods at the edge of Covey's property.

Good. Head clearing, feet moving. I can do it.

Frederick was almost to the edge of the field when Covey spotted him and jumped on his horse, howling in rage. Frederick dashed into the forest; he knew it well, having spent a great deal of time chopping firewood there.

When Frederick's strength gave out, he flung himself into a large thicket, remaining motionless while Covey thundered through the underbrush, shouting threats and poking the bushes with his whip. He grew impatient; his crop would never get threshed this way! Covey went home, sure that his wounded, hungry slave would finally give up and come home, too.

Frederick waited patiently for a half hour after his master left. Then he made his way through the thick woods, hoping a rattlesnake would not strike at him. None did, but thorns tore at his worn clothes, and mosquitoes attacked his scabby back and bleeding head injury with a vengeance. Frederick walked as long as he could, then rested, then walked again. He had decided his only hope was to reach St. Michaels and somehow convince Thomas Auld that Covey was damaging his property. Frederick stumbled into Auld's store just as he was closing. Captain Auld could not believe his eyes. Frederick's hair was matted with blood, his arms and legs raked by thorns, his clothes shredded. He told Auld about his sudden illness and Covey's mistreatment.

"Please," begged Frederick, "please, Master. Rent me to another farmer, and I will work hard. But don't send me back to Mr. Covey. He wants to kill me, and then you will have nothing."

He believes me, thought Frederick, seeing the shock on his face. *He believes me.* A tiny flame of hope lit in his heart.

But as Frederick described the chase through the woods, Captain Auld's eyes hardened.

"Impossible. You should never have run away from Mr. Covey. He is a good Christian man, so you must have been avoiding work so that he had to punish you. I made an agreement with him. And I would have to return the entire year's amount of your wages that he already paid me."

Thomas gave Frederick a large dose of Epsom salts, the universal medication for slaves' illnesses, and told him to spend the night in the kitchen.

"You will walk back and apologize to Mr. Covey tomorrow morning."

Frederick did not respond to Eliza's cries of gladness and horror when he entered. He did not care if she washed his wounds or not.

My God, my God. Why have You forsaken me?

"I have no food allowance for you," said Rowena Auld. "Mr. Covey is supposed to feed and board you for the year. That is the agreement."

Eliza had nothing to share; she was going without food herself in order to feed her children that day. "Fed, I'm so sorry."

Frederick nodded and touched her cheek gently. He left Auld's house feeling he was on his way to hell. *No man cares for my soul.* He had slept little on the hard floor, and his wounds stung and seeped as he made his way slowly down the main road of Bayside.

As Frederick approached the house, a figure suddenly leaped out at him from behind a fence. *Covey!*

Frederick ran to the woods. Covey followed, but soon gave up the search. He knew Frederick could not go back to Auld's house; Thomas's messenger had arrived and informed Covey of Auld's decision. Frederick was too intelligent, Covey reasoned, to attempt an escape to freedom up North; he'd never make it off the peninsula, now the community was aware of his earlier bid for liberty.

He loves to eat, that boy, thought Covey. *He'll come home soon enough. And I'll be ready for 'im.*

Frederick lay in the woods, too exhausted to contemplate the future. His empty stomach clenched like a fist because of the Epsom salts. He lay on his back and waited for the sympathetic darkness to hide him.

What should I do? he thought. *What can I do? Maybe God only listens to white men's prayers.* Hunger raked at him like the thorn bushes. He crept closer to the main road.

Footsteps! Had Covey changed his mind and decided to pursue him at night?

But they belonged to a black man. It was Sandy Jenkins, a hired slave on his way to see his wife, a free woman who lived in her own cabin on Pot Pie Neck. Frederick had heard that Sandy was a compassionate man. At any rate, he had to trust someone. He stepped out onto the main road.

"Fed! You still run from Covey?" the man asked.

"I can't go back, Sandy. Not yet, anyway."

Sandy nodded. He risked thirty-nine lashes, according to Maryland law, and his wife could be imprisoned, if they gave aid to a rebellious slave. He did not hesitate.

"Y'all look plumb tuckered out," said Sandy. "Come with me, and we find you somethin' to eat."

He put his arm around the tall, swaying figure and helped him down the road.

"You take this here root and hide it in your clothes," said Sandy. "I always carry it, and nobody beat me since I got it."

Frederick regarded his host with amusement, but agreed to take the root. He would have carried a boulder, if Sandy had told him to. Despite the lateness of their arrival, his wife immediately stirred up a huge ash cake for Frederick, who had not eaten in thirty-six hours. The coarse bread had never tasted so good. They gathered together a soft pile of straw, and Frederick slept dreamlessly. The Sunday morning dawned and hope with it. He would go back to Covey, he decided. He could not endanger the Jenkinses any longer. *But,* Frederick told himself, *I will not let him flog me.*

The idea grew in his head as he bade his hosts good-bye and resolutely set out. *God doesn't want me to hurt him, and I won't. But I will not let him flog me.*

Frederick arrived at the farm just as the Coveys were leaving for Sunday services.

"Would you shoo the pigs out of the barn, Frederick?" asked Covey pleasantly.

Frederick nodded incredulously.

"Have a good Sabbath," said Covey as the wagon passed.

Frederick poked the recalcitrant pigs, then lay down under an oak tree beside the barn to rest. Could Sandy's root have had a magical effect on his master?

More likely he's on his Sunday behavior, thought Frederick cynically. *Tomorrow morning we'll see.*

"Easy, girl," said Frederick. He curried the farm horse gently; she wasn't as beautiful as Colonel Lloyd's thoroughbreds, but she worked hard and deserved good treatment. He fetched some oats.

His right foot went skyward! Covey leapt from his hiding place in a stall, grabbed Frederick's leg, and tried to tie a rope around his feet. Frederick flipped him to the dirt floor and held Covey in a vise.

"Help, Bill! He's got me!" shouted Covey.

His cousin charged into the barn, only to receive a kick from Frederick. Bill Hughes backed out of the barn and did not return, despite Covey's cries.

The two opponents grappled for over two hours, neither giving in. But hard farm work had changed Frederick from a string-bean boy into a powerful young man; Covey was strong, but the farmer was no match for his desperate field hand.

"Smith! Get him off me!"

Bill Smith, the other hired slave, had just returned from visiting his family over Sunday. He looked confused.

"Mr. Covey, sir? What did you say?"

"I say, GET HIM OFF ME!"

"Mr. Covey, your bull is headed for your neighbor's field. I better go git him."

Smith left. When Covey tried to grab a heavy wooden stick and strike Frederick, he seized it and threw Covey into a manure pile.

"Caroline, grab him!"

But Caroline, who had just arrived with pails of table scraps for the hogs, stood immobile, her stomach protruding under her worn dress. Covey had locked her in the kitchen shed every night with Bill Smith until she became pregnant.

"No," she said.

Covey, enraged, struck at her with filthy hands until she ran back to the house. The two combatants struggled once more.

Finally Covey loosened his grip on Frederick. "Go to work," he commanded wearily. "If you had not resisted, you would not have been whipped."

Frederick tried not to laugh. He had not been whipped at all! He had strength to spare, and an exhilaration that easily out-glowed his earlier despair.

Covey never again tried to flog Frederick, although he later whipped Caroline for her refusal to help him. He railed at him, especially when Frederick intentionally slowed in his work, but he did not use his whip. Frederick pondered why Covey did not find someone else stronger to give him the customary thirty-nine lashes for running away.

Perhaps, he thought, *if folks find out a sixteen-year-old beat him, they won't think he's such a wonderful nigger-breaker.*

Frederick walked down the Bayside road the last time on Christmas Day. He would never go to Covey's again.

Eliza and her little ones, Henny, and Priscilla welcomed Frederick to the Auld kitchen for the small holiday feast that Thomas gave the slaves once a year, much to Rowena's disgust. Compared to Covey's, the Auld household was heaven. But he would remain there only a week. Thomas had hired him out once more to William Freeland who, unlike Covey, was known as a kind, patient master.

We'll see how kind Freeland is, thought Frederick.

To his surprise, William Freeland gave him plenty of work, but provided abundant food, rest, and medical care. He was later to say that Freeland was the best master he ever had besides himself.[4] His slaves actually possessed leisure time to pursue their own interests. Frederick began to read again.

Freeland's neighbors, Rev. Daniel Weeden and Rev. Regby Hopkins, sickened Frederick with their treatment of their slaves. Rev. Hopkins made it a practice to whip a slave or two every Monday as preventive medicine for bad behavior among his workers. Both were fervent preachers and had reputations for profound piety, but Frederick grew increasingly disenchanted with their double standard of behavior and that of the established church in general.

His own master, unlike them, did not claim any faith at all. But he did not object to Frederick's cultivating his own, and when Frederick once again began teaching a slave Sunday school, William Freeland simply looked the other way. Frederick and his friends were wise enough, however, to keep their classes secret; Freeland might not object to their activities, but certainly his neighbors would.

It's amazing, Frederick mused, *that in Christian America young blacks can spend their Sundays getting drunk, playing games, or even fighting, and there are no objections from whites. But learning to read the Scriptures—that is not allowed.*

78

Frederick's students met under trees, behind barns, and in the woods. When the weather grew cold, a freedman offered his home for classes, and Frederick taught over forty pupils three nights a week. Area blacks were in awe of Frederick because of his fight with Covey; they were ready to listen to him.

Frederick's year at William Freeland's passed quickly; Christmas came, and Frederick was amazed at Freeland's generosity to his slaves. His master provided sumptuous meals and plenty of applejack, encouraged games and contests, and distributed gifts. For the week between Christmas and New Year's, the black workers on his farm celebrated with singing, dancing, fiddle-playing, and "juba (jubilee) beating," in which a drummer beat on a barrel top while singers spontaneously composed songs to his rhythms.

These festivities, he found, were routine on Southern plantations; Frederick had happened to live where they were not. Frederick ran races, bested his friends in wrestling, and danced with pretty girls. He became roaring drunk on applejack for the first time, and enjoyed the exaggerated sense of power it gave him.

"Honored chairman, I beg to address the assembly!" Frederick thundered, using lines he had studied in the *Columbian Orator.*

"Fed, you ain't a-dressin' nobody," said his friend John Harris, " 'cept the hogs." The two teenagers woke up after their drinking binge to find themselves facing a huge, angry mother pig.

Many women used their Christmas vacation to make corn brooms, mats, horse collars, and baskets for sale. Men hunted for game which supplemented their diets. Freeland, unlike many Southern masters, did not discourage these industrious activities.

Why would they dislike it? Frederick asked himself. *Why would they rather bet on which slave can drink the most than cheer those on who want to better their families?* He observed closely as the slaves grew tired of the seemingly endless partying and returned to their usual hard work almost with relief. *Christmas is a sop, a deliberate attempt to placate slaves,* thought Frederick. *Without Christmas, the South would explode with rebellion. It gives us just enough fun to live through the hard times. And when we are done with our time of debauchery, they say to us, see what too much freedom does to you? You need us to help keep you in line.*

Frederick began to consider abstinence from alcohol.

He spent most of New Year's Day 1836, thinking deeply about his own slavery. Thomas Auld had hired him out to William Freeland for another year. He had plenty of food, clothing and shelter, time to read and study, and stimulating opportunities to help fellow slaves grow spiritually and academically.

For now.

What if Thomas Auld dies, and I am sold down South? He knew he was considered valuable property; he could easily do a man's heavy work.

What if he grows angry with me and sends me back to Covey?

What if he keeps me, and I grow old in Rowena's kitchen, living on half a peck of cornmeal a week, unable to read my Bible without hiding?

What if he decides that I shall live my life out on Mr. Freeland's farm? Will I hoe his ground, content to be a slave forever?

"No," said Frederick to the sullen sky.

"It is time."

seven

F ed, how we get to Pennsylvania?" John rubbed his hands over the fire as he and Frederick's other students took a break from their books.

"We take a canoe, paddle past Maryland and Delaware, then go north to Pennsylvania."

"Ain't New York City free?"

"Sure is, Henry." Frederick smiled at the brothers.

"Mebbe we go there, too."

"Maybe." Frederick did not want to admit that he had no idea where New York City was, or how to get there. He did not even know that the free state of New York existed. "But I think our first plan is the best. We have to stay away from land so people will think we're fishing for our masters and won't question us as they would if we were traveling on land."

Frederick, John and Henry Harris, Sandy Jenkins, Charles Roberts, and Frederick's young uncle Henry Bailey had talked of freedom for months. But now Frederick's New Year's resolution fired the young black men with enthusiasm to escape.

"We have to collect supplies for the journey," said Frederick. "Henry, you must make sure that Mr. Hambleton's biggest canoe is ready for us to use by the week before Easter."

The boys never did get back to their books. The fire died, and still they talked of their dream.

"It's late, boys," said Sandy, the oldest of the group, who was in his early twenties. "We better go a'fore somebody notice we gone."

"He's right," agreed Frederick. The boys clasped each other's hands.

"Slavery is an affront to God every hour," intoned Frederick.

"A-men!" they chorused.

"Give us liberty or give us death!"

"A-men!"

The boys waved good-bye to Willie Hayes, the freedman in whose house they met.

They continued planning throughout the winter. Sometimes the sessions were full of the joy of their anticipated freedom. Other nights were somber as they realized the enormity of their task and feared the dangers of the unknown.

"Reckon they'll follow us with hound dogs?" asked Henry Bailey. He had seen a group of slave hunters pursue a runaway through a swamp with a pack of howling animals.

"How are dogs gonna follow our canoe in the Bay?" asked Frederick. The other boys chuckled, and Henry grinned ashamedly.

"But they might follow us when we land on shore."

"By the time they figure out where we are, our trail will be stone cold."

"Can we carry 'nuff food to keep us all till we in Pennsylvania? Takin' it from farms would leave a trail, and we sho' cain't buy none." John Harris always asked the practical questions.

"They's lots of rattlers in the woods!" Charles was terrified of snakes.

"There were lots of them in the wilderness, too, when Moses and the Israelites ran from Pharaoh," answered Frederick. "But God Almighty took care of them in the desert, and He will take care of us."

"Fed," said Sandy seriously, "I done had a dream last night that makes me wonder if this is a good idea."

All the boys paused.

"I seen a big bird got you in his claws, Fed, and all kinds of birds, big ones, little ones, tryin' to peck yo' eyes out. They peck at yo' head, yo' arms, then all of a sudden, all them birds fly away to the southwest, carry you with 'em."

"You've been drinkin' too much applejack, Sandy," said Frederick, trying to laugh off his friend's concern.

"Mebbe it mean they sell you South," said Sandy.

Silence.

"It's a warnin'. I cain't do this, Fed."

"Sandy, we can't let every little nightmare scare us out of our freedom. We want you with us when we go North. Think how grand it will be. Freedom to be a man, not an animal!"

"I got to go, Fed," said Sandy. He left the room quietly as the rest stared with open mouths.

"We cain't leave Sandy here!"

"Sandy cared for me when nobody else did," said Frederick sadly. "I wish he would come. But since he won't, we got to think of ourselves. For one thing, the canoe won't be so crowded, and we'll make better time."

The rest had to agree with this logic. After Frederick had made several more rousing speeches and clasped hands with his friends, the group chorused "A-men!" with their usual vigor.

The conspirators planned their escape for Saturday, April 2, because most slave masters gave their workers a holiday on Easter weekend that often lasted into Monday. Slaves visited other farms at this time. Their absence might not be noticed until Monday night, or perhaps even Tuesday, giving them a good head start. Frederick kept the boys hard at work on details and continued to inspire them with Exodus and speeches from the *Columbian Orator.* He carefully penned and distributed the bogus passes that declared each could travel to Baltimore for Easter break.

Suddenly, it was the last week of March. The young men met clandestinely almost every day, holding hands and swearing they would have their freedom or die in the attempt. "Canaan-bound, we won't stay much longer down here!" they sang at their work.

Frederick tingled with excitement that increased every day. He tried not to smile too much as he hoed young tobacco plants. Nighttime, however, often brought fears and sleeplessness.

Frederick awoke that Saturday, his anxiety at a fever pitch. He and Sandy spread manure in the fields, as usual. They would work into the afternoon before Frederick and the others met on William Hambleton's farm for their evening adventure. He tried to feel ecstatic. Wasn't this the day he had lived for? Suddenly Frederick his felt his mother's presence.

No, Frederick. No.

"We've been betrayed, Sandy," said Frederick. "I can feel my mother telling me."

Sandy nodded. "Crazy, but I do, too."

The breakfast horn sounded, and the two had no choice but to walk to the farmhouse as they always did. But Frederick saw three white men on horseback down the lane, followed by two blacks, their arms bound. One of the white men was William Hambleton, a sedate old man who never galloped. He was galloping now to the house.

"Where is your master?" he spat at Frederick.

"Behind the barn," answered Frederick. His worst fears were realized. Two of the whites were Constables Tom Graham and Ned Hambleton. The two black men tied with heavy ropes were Charles Roberts and Henry Bailey.

Hambleton seized Frederick and wrenched his hands behind him, while Graham bound him. The constables each wore pistols; Frederick knew that resistance was useless. He hung his head. Everything was useless.

"We're gonna take you and your slave friends to Easton for questioning," said Hambleton. "Thought you could just run off?" He slapped Frederick, hard.

"We gotta get the others," said Graham. They pushed Frederick through the door and grabbed John and Henry Harrison, who had just sat down for breakfast.

"Cross your hands," snapped Hambleton. John reluctantly did so, but Henry clasped his into fists.

"No."

"Open your hands and cross 'em!" demanded Graham.

"I'll blow the heart out of you!" Hambleton yanked his pistol out.

Henry's eyes burned. "You can't kill me but once. Shoot and be damned! I won't be tied!"

The two white men wrestled fiercely with Henry. William Hambleton and Freeland returned from the barn to help beat Henry senseless before they could manage to tie his hands.

Frederick watched helplessly. *We all said we would resist any attempt at capture. We all said we would die rather than lose our freedom. But Henry's the only one that did it.*

He felt like collapsing from sheer hopelessness.

The passes. *The passes.*

Frederick slowly felt in his pocket with his bound hand. There it was, the forged pass that was to help win his liberty. He had not fought valiantly like Henry. But Frederick would not let them find this evidence on him. While the men struggled and swore, Frederick edged closer to the fire.

There it goes. It was the only sense of satisfaction the morning had given him. If only he could manage a way to get rid of all the others. . . .

"Yellow devil! It was that yellow devil got John and Henry to do it. They're our boys, born right on this farm!" Freeland's mother, Betsey, raged at Frederick as she wet Henry's broken face with a cold cloth and brought the brothers biscuits.

Frederick fixed flaming eyes on her, and Betsey ran from the kitchen screaming, "Yellow devil!"

Freeland said nothing. He followed the constables, who took Frederick and John outside.

"Git on your feet," said Hambleton to Henry.

The battered young man struggled to stand, then held his head high as he left the only home he had ever known.

The slave masters and constables mounted their horses. The young black men, bound tightly together, stumbled behind them.

Sandy Jenkins watched the ugly procession until it was a speck in the distance.

"Fed."

Frederick had stared at the dust as the boys marched.

Had someone whispered his name?

"Fed."

Henry Harris looked straight ahead, and his lips barely moved behind the biscuit he held to them. But Henry spoke to Frederick!

"What do we do with the passes?"

"Eat them with your biscuits," answered Frederick.

Henry munched slowly with his bruised mouth and elbowed John, who elbowed Charles. Henry gave Frederick a quick wink and continued his plodding gait. Frederick was overcome with relief and gratitude. Henry still considered him their leader! He did not hold their situation against him, even though he had fought bravely and Frederick had given in to their captors. As they trudged the three miles to St. Michaels, the others occasionally glanced his way. No anger. No resentment. Frederick could hardly believe that a man could have friends like his!

"Don't admit anything," said Frederick to Henry. He nodded imperceptibly and passed the order to John.

The group entered St. Michaels; children pointed, and women came out their front doors. Loafers in Thomas Auld's store rejoiced to see some excitement in the village.

"What is the meaning of this?" Auld demanded.

"Your slave tried to get mine to run off," answered William Hambleton, his plump face reddening. "Trouble-makers like him ought to be horsewhipped, then burnt."

Thomas Auld ranted and raved at Frederick, but his too-vehement anger told Frederick that his master was not sure that Hambleton and the constables had any true indication of his guilt.

"We were all at work when they bound us," asserted Frederick loudly. "We had no intention of running away. Why should we try to escape from such kind masters?"

Why, indeed! Frederick knew this very question would puzzle all the white men.

"They had forged passes on 'em," asserted William Hambleton.

"Please search us," urged Frederick, "and you will find no such thing."

All the boys submitted meekly to the search. When it produced nothing, Auld and Hambleton shouted at them and each other. Frederick listened closely; it appeared their owners had only one witness against the boys.

"Please," Frederick begged, "if someone has aught against us, let him speak plainly to us. We wish to know who would bring such a terrible charge against us."

"That is impossible," Auld blustered, "but we have so much proof of your crime that it would be enough to hang you, if you'd killed someone."

"But no one's been murdered!" cried Frederick. "And no one's run away. We are all here. What wrong has been done?"

"Shut up," said Ned Hambleton. He and Graham shoved the boys outside while Auld, Freeland, and Hambleton argued earnestly. Frederick could hear little of it. Finally, they joined the constables.

"Take 'em to Easton," said Auld, "and we'll see."

The white men mounted their horses once more, and Frederick and his friends followed them on another long trek.

"He ought to be hanged!"

"He ought to have the hide whipped off his back!"

"Burn 'im! *Burn!*"

Frederick tried not to shiver. John and Henry, Charles and Henry Bailey occasionally risked a kind look his direction. But angered whites recognized Frederick as the ringleader. They lined the road, screaming insults and calling for his death. Others laughed at him, mocking the "highfalutin nigger" who had to tramp through twelve miles of dust in the afternoon sun. Only a few blacks who hoed the fields dared send him a sympathetic glance. Other field hands cast furious looks his way; his escape attempt would only make their lives harder, Frederick knew. But he refused to quail before any of them.

The birds. . . , Frederick thought. *These vultures are too much like Sandy's birds. Sandy. SANDY.* Frederick almost vomited.

Only Sandy had known the details of their escape plan. Only Sandy had known about the false passes. And he had pulled out of the scheme not long before it was to take place. How had their captors known exactly who was involved? They had even known about the canoe. Who had told them?

Frederick forced himself to keep walking, eyes fixed stonily ahead. Sandy had even risked a whipping to save him from Covey. Sandy was their friend. Would he have turned them in for money to buy his own freedom? No, Sandy could not have done it.

Where is the God of justice and mercy? Why do You allow them to trample us in the dust?

"Why—why—why," the very rhythm of the horses' hooves tormented Frederick. Another mile of misery. Frederick knew they were not far from Easton. What awaited them there? Thirty-nine lashes? A lynch mob with nooses?

"He shall save the children of the needy, and shall break in pieces the oppressor." Psalm 72:4, which Uncle Lawson had taught him in Baltimore, ran through Frederick's mind. A tiny ray of hope shone inside him.

89

That's me, Lord. I am needy. I need You right now.

Frederick stared in disbelief. Sheriff Joseph Graham did not beat the captives upon their arrival in Easton. He directed Frederick and John and Henry Harris into one large, clean cell, and Charles and Henry Bailey into another. He brought them bowls of thin, watery soup to eat, but it was better soup than Thomas Auld's. Frederick lay on the floor, grateful for the cool evening breeze through the black lattice windows. He felt better physically, but his whole being mourned the loss of his freedom. Even his friends' comforting presence did little to lift the dark fog.

I'll be sold down South, he thought. Henry Bailey's innocent dark eyes searched for his.

"Fed?"

Frederick kept his eyes tightly closed so the younger boy would believe he was sleeping.

Old Hambleton will sell Henry, too; they'll sell all of them down South, and it's all my fault.

The next day was Sunday, so the boys saw only church-goers pass their windows. But Monday morning brought a flurry of activity across the street at Sol Lowe's hotel. They watched men in gaudy suits demand their coffee and eggs. They were slave traders, Frederick knew, who had heard about the boys' arrival. Plantation owners shunned them as white trash gotten rich; slaves feared them like a deadly disease. Frederick wished he were a waiter; they heard all the slave traders' news, and would know their fate.

"Let me see your arm, boy." The jail door burst open, and a large, grinning man in a bright green waistcoat breezed into Frederick's cell. "You're a big 'un."

He smiled unpleasantly as he felt Frederick's arms and legs as if he were a prize stallion. It took every ounce of control he had to keep from flattening the slave trader.

Several other traders followed him, all gabbling and jeering at the boys: "Where did y'all think y'all were goin? Are you havin' a nice holiday? Think you'd like me as your master?" They wrenched open their mouths, pulled their shirts off, and sized the captives up. Frederick felt as if he were surrounded by a group of evil spirits straight from hell, most of them reeking with whiskey.

Henry Bailey tried not to cringe in terror. *My fault,* Frederick thought. *My fault.*

"You," said the large man, "the big yella-skinned one. How would you like me for your master?"

Frederick ignored him.

"If I had you," the slave trader thrust his sneering face so close that Frederick inhaled his stinking breath, "if I had you, I would cut the devil out of you pretty quick."

The other traders laughed uproariously. Frederick and his friends remained silent.

"Boys," said Sheriff Graham, "your masters are here to take you home."

The young black men stared at each other in amazement.

"Mr. Hambleton is waitin' outside for Henry and Charles. And Mr. Freeland come to take John and Henry. Y'all look smart; they been kind to you boys. You, Fed, you gotta stay." The sheriff could not suppress a look of sympathy as he saw the hope in Frederick's eyes fade.

Charles, Henry Bailey and John clasped Frederick's hand, but could not disguise their elation. But Henry Harris only left his cell when the sheriff gave him a push, saying, "Y'all better git out while the gittin's good, boy!"

"Go on, Henry," whispered Frederick. "Don't worry about me."

"But, Fed," protested his friend.

"Go back and take care of the others," insisted Frederick. "I'll see you some day in Canaan land."

Henry's eyes filled with tears and rage, but he nodded and left Frederick, who calmly waved until the door clanged shut.

Alone.

Frederick dropped to his prison floor, drowning in darkness, even though the morning sunshine sang through the metal bars on his windows.

"Fed, wake up."

Frederick stirred groggily. He had found that sleeping numbed his pain like a narcotic; it passed the hours that seemed to straggle endlessly by. He had only been in prison a week, and it seemed a lifetime.

"Captain Auld, he come to get you," said Sheriff Graham, grinning. "See? He didn't forget you, Fed."

Auld? Why would Auld come for him? The slave traders had visited every day; facing their taunts was much harder alone than when his friends were there. Every day he expected one of them to slap chains on his ankles and haul him to the dock to sail to Louisiana and the deadly sugar cane fields. Did Auld want to whip Frederick himself before he got rid of his troublesome slave forever?

"Go get in the wagon, Fed," was all Thomas Auld said.

They rode through town, Frederick hunched miserably in the back, all too aware of the smug expressions of the villagers.

"I aim to sell you to a friend of mine in Alabama," said Thomas. "Maybe he'll free you one of these days, maybe seven, eight years from now. Take care of the horses, then see what they got for you to do in the kitchen."

Frederick did not want to go indoors; the green grass between his toes and the fiery sunset were too wonderful to waste.

Eliza burst from the kitchen door and threw her arms around her brother. Frederick was glad to see her, thankful to be alive, and relieved to have escaped his master's whip—so far. But he was also wary. He had never heard of a kind master in Alabama, especially one that bought slaves with the intention of freeing them. It made no sense at all. Frederick guessed Auld had a much more ominous fate in mind for him and simply wanted to raise false hopes.

Thomas said no more to him that day, but the next morning ordered him to ride with him down to the dock.

"I'm sending you to Hugh's again," said Captain Auld. "I want you to learn a trade, and if you conduct yourself properly, I'll free you when you're twenty-five."

Frederick stared at the man in total disbelief. Back to Baltimore? This was too much like the sweet dreams that seduced him when he was still in jail, only to torment him when he awoke. Where was the master that had sent him back to Covey's, hungry and bleeding, with only another brutal beating to anticipate? Where was the religious hypocrite that beat poor Henny senseless and quoted Scripture while doing it? Frederick searched Auld's face. He had no way of knowing that Auld had left him in jail not only to learn his lesson, but also to protect him from Hambleton and others. They had threatened to shoot Frederick when Auld had decided not to sell him down South, as was proper. Later, Frederick's cousin Tom would tell him that Auld had walked the floor sleeplessly the night before his release, trying to decide what to do with him. The slave traders had bartered vigorously for Frederick, but Captain Auld had ignored them all.

Baltimore. Frederick felt tears surge against his eyelids and hope press against the walls of suspicion he had built inside. *Liar. Liar.*

But Captain Auld put Frederick on a sloop. "Remember, Fed."

Frederick only stared. The boat pulled into the river's current and toward the glorious, glistening Chesapeake Bay.

eight

C ome, you sweet lambs of God!"
    Frederick pursed his lips in an oily smile and
    gestured limply. His "congregation," several young
black men and women, tried to stifle their laughter.
Frederick stood on the tips of his toes and stared glassily in
a perfect imitation of Rev. Humphrey Simpson, a prominent
Baltimore minister.

"The Shepherd will welcome not only white lambs, but
He even lets little black lambs find their way to the heavenly fold," intoned Frederick in a high, maudlin voice.

Frederick's friend William Lloyd began to move toward
the "pulpit," wiping feigned tears with a large red bandanna, only to be interrupted by the indignant "reverend":
"What do you mean, boy, by coming to the front of the
church? Everybody knows the Bible says the black lambs
are supposed to come in the back gate of heaven!"

Addie Sims giggled hysterically until her friends had to
pound her on the back.

"Mr. Bailey, you should be 'shamed of yourself!" she

remonstrated with a grin. "I don't know if I can sit through Rev. Simpson's sermons without laughing!"

"He deserves to be laughed at, Miss Sims," Frederick said, suddenly serious. "Rev. Simpson does appear to believe we are somewhat human, which is more than most white ministers do. I grant him that. But he thinks Negroes are an afterthought of the Creator; his actions say we are not made in the image of God, as he himself is."

William, Joseph Lewis, Henry Rolles, and Samuel Dougherty, all members of the East Baltimore Mental Improvement Society, faced Frederick expectantly. Addie, Ellen Goode, and Anna Murray waited for the powerful oratory they knew would come.

"Woe unto you, scribes and Pharisees, hypocrites!" said Frederick, his voice deepening and his eyes ablaze. "All their works they do for to be seen of men. . .and love the uppermost rooms at feasts, and the chief seats in the synagogues. . . . For they loved the praise of men more than the praise of God." (Matthew 23:5–6, John 12:43) They would be shocked at the proposition of fellowshipping with a sheep-stealer; and at the same time they hug to their communion a man-stealer, and brand me with being an infidel, if I find fault with them for it.[1] If our Redeemer died for Negroes, too, then how can such things go on in Christian America in the churches that bear His name?"

Frederick spoke passionately; although his mind and heart were truly full of his convictions, part of him watched the mesmerizing effect his rhetoric had on his listeners. Anna, a quiet young woman with rich, walnut skin and a fawn's dark eyes, warmed him with her gentle smile.

Baltimore was not the heaven Frederick envisioned during his days in St. Michaels. Sophia Auld had another baby,

Edward, and was often irritable. Frederick had done a man's work the three years he was gone; he was no longer interested in quieting crying little ones or scrubbing pots for Miss Sophia. Tommy, his adoring little "brother," was now an adolescent; he regarded Frederick with an air of superiority that grated on him.

Hugh, however, paid attention to him for the first time. The gangly boy had become a young man with broad shoulders and heavily muscled arms. Unmistakable intelligence and restless energy gleamed in his eyes. He might become an excellent source of income if he were trained appropriately. Hugh apprenticed Frederick as a caulker in William Gardiner's shipyard.

But times had changed in Baltimore. For years blacks and whites had labored in the shipyards with little regard for either's color or status. An economic depression and the resulting shortage of work caused white workers to resent the free blacks that competed for jobs. Blacks, on the other hand, were hostile to the ever-increasing stream of Irish immigrants who flooded Baltimore and took jobs that traditionally went to blacks: manual shipyard and railroad work, draying, and domestic service. The carpenters at Frederick's shipyard demanded that all free blacks be fired from their jobs. William Gardiner, desperate to finish two large warships, the *Fourth of July* and the *Independence,* on time, agreed. Frederick was the only black retained, because he was a slave, and his wages went to a white master.

Despite his slavery, he was a reminder of all the freed blacks who were out to destroy the Irishmen's American dream. He had to follow orders any of the hundred white men gave him. "Fred, come help me saw this beam." "Halloo! Bring me some water." "If you move, I'll knock you through the wall!" It was a frustrating eight months, as Frederick had little opportunity to learn any caulking.

The carpenters also encouraged the other apprentices to harass Frederick. Frederick ignored the racial slurs that were part of his everyday work life, but one day when Edward North tried to punch him, Frederick picked him up easily and deposited him in the ocean. He got into several shoving matches with the other apprentices, but their respect for his physical strength kept these from developing into outright fights.

Until one day.

Frederick went to work whistling; he truly enjoyed construction work. His way, however, was blocked by Edward, who held a brick, grinning. Before Frederick could react, Bill Stewart and Tom Humphreys closed in on him from the side, and Ned Hays struck him from behind with a handspike, a hefty iron bar used to position timbers. They pummeled him with their fists. One kicked him in the eye, and a scarlet stream of blood squirted all over the sawdust floor. Frightened, the apprentices scattered. Frederick, still bleeding, grasped the handspike and tried to follow them.

"Kill the nigger! He struck a white boy!" The workers closed in around him, but no one touched Frederick. Finally, they went back to their jobs, while Frederick painfully made his way to the Aulds' home.

"Freddy! What happened to you!" Sophia Auld almost wept. "Sit here!" She wet soft rags and gently bathed Frederick's bloody, bruised face, covering the wounded eye with a piece of raw beef.

"How could they do such a thing to our Freddy?"

The tight knot of rage in Frederick began to relax under Sophia's motherly hands. Her eyes filled with tears of sympathy; she seemed like the "Miss Sophia" he had adored as a child.

Hugh flew into a rage when informed of Frederick's injuries.

"Idiots!" he roared. "Imbeciles!" He let loose a string of profanity that sent Sophia and the children running for the parlor. "I'll have the whole lot of them arrested!" Frederick enjoyed Hugh's fervency, although he suspected it was anger based on mistreatment of his property. Hugh told Frederick to rest until he was able to accompany him to see a magistrate.

Frederick relished the quiet day or two, despite his stiffness and swollen, painful eye. Sophia fussed over him and refused to let him do any work.

Hugh and Frederick walked to the office of Esquire Watson on Bond Street.

Hugh wrathfully told the magistrate what had happened, showed him Frederick's wounds, and waited to hear the magistrate respond with an immediate order for the arrest of the criminals.

"How many men witnessed this?" asked Watson.

"At least fifty," answered Hugh impatiently.

"Unless you can produce at least one white witness, I cannot, by Maryland law, prosecute anyone."

"Witnesses! Witnesses?" said Hugh, his face beginning to purple. "Look at his eye, his face! Can you not see what was done!"

"Nevertheless," said the dry little man, "I cannot commence with charges until you find one white man who will testify on your slave's behalf."

Hugh stormed out of the office with Frederick, who tried not to wince with every step. They both knew that Hugh would never find a witness at Gardiner's.

"You are not going back to that den of fools," said Hugh. "You would learn very little there, anyway." He ended Frederick's apprenticeship and found him a position at Walter Price's shipyard, where he himself now worked.

Work was still difficult at times, but few men cared to accost Hugh, who could beat most challengers into a pulp, as Frederick knew too well. He loved watching awkward piles of logs magically changed into proud sailing ships. He worked hard at his trade and became known as an industrious, skillful journeyman who earned top wages for his master.

As Frederick watched the white workmen pocket their wages each week, his own situation rankled deep within him. "I was now getting. . .a dollar and fifty cents per day. I contracted for it, worked for it, earned it, collected it; it was paid to me, and it was *rightfully* my own; and yet, upon every returning Saturday night, this money—my own hard earnings, every cent of it—was demanded of me, and taken from me by Master Hugh. . . . The right to take my earnings was the right of the robber."[2]

I must be free. Frederick's mind was as busy as his hands. One day, Frederick thought, he would approach Hugh about finding his own quarters in Baltimore. He would contract his own jobs, pay his own room and board, and give a fixed amount to Hugh each week. Frederick knew many slaves in the area had similar agreements with their masters. He had already approached Thomas Auld about the idea when he had visited a few months before. Auld rejected his proposal indignantly.

"I have done for you what no other master has," said Thomas icily. "I am sure that you are simply concocting a scheme to run away. If you do run away, I *will* find you, Fed." His eyes bored into Frederick's, then softened. "Let us have no more such nonsense. Do as you are told, and I will take care of you."

Frederick seethed with resentment, but consoled himself with the idea that he would approach Hugh later. Two months later he did.

"I'll think on it," Hugh grunted. Frederick was beside himself with joy. At least Hugh, knowing Thomas's opinion, did not outright reject his idea.

The more Hugh thought about Frederick's proposal, the more appealing it sounded. Hugh's small house was full to bursting, and Sophia was pregnant again; there was little room for a moody, defiant young giant who ate as much as the rest of the family combined. Frederick would guarantee Hugh an income, regardless of his own employment. Although Hugh's small inner voice protested that such freedom would only whet Frederick's appetite for it, the prospect of the easing of his financial burden and having his home to himself was too strong a temptation for Hugh. He consented.

Frederick walked to his tiny room in the attic of a run-down boardinghouse. He stripped the bed and took the grimy covers down to the wharf, where he beat them on the rocks and laid them on a grassy area to dry. Tonight he would sleep, undisturbed by fussy babies. He would miss Miss Sophia's cooking, but not her everlasting nagging. He would only have to see Hugh weekly! *Freedom to choose a cup of coffee or tea for breakfast, freedom to meet my friends, freedom to leave my Bible lying on my bed, freedom to simply be—no questions asked.*

John Auburn's saloon, alive with lamplight and noise, beckoned to Frederick as he carried his fresh bed linens home. Most shipyard workers considered Auburn's a required stop on the way home; his grog was famous for its flavor and potency. Although Frederick would have no doubt met friends in the small, packed room reserved for blacks in the back, he decided against it.

This small liberty I have means more than a chance to drink and carouse. It means that I can plan for my true freedom. Frederick made six to nine dollars weekly, depending on the availability of jobs. He had to give Hugh three dollars a week and support himself.

But the rest I will save for my escape.

Day, night—Frederick would work whenever he could.

He was up early every morning; if he did not have a job that day, he searched the shipyards relentlessly until he found one. He willingly worked as a laborer in the evenings. For a time, he even acted as a butler and also accompanied a family's small children to a school run by Mrs. Elizabeth Wells, where he was introduced to the violin, an instrument he loved all his life.

Frederick's long hours did not, however, interfere with his devotion to the East Baltimore Mental Improvement Society. The gifted young freedmen helped ease the loss of Frederick's friends in Talbot County. They read and discussed many issues of the day, but the prevalent one was, of course, slavery. Frederick polished his speaking skills and taught his friends all he learned from the *Columbian Orator.* They gave him access to information that often was denied him as a slave. Young women, too, like Anna Murray, often attended meetings. *Addie is far more vivacious than Anna,* Frederick thought. *Ellen is lovely in a limpid, dreamy way. But there is something about Anna. She is always serene, no matter how hotheaded our meetings become. She listens intently, but rarely speaks. When she does, it is like a cool breeze on a scorching afternoon. And she makes the most incredible cinnamon buns!* Frederick began calling on Anna, who worked as a domestic for a postmaster in Fells Point. To his delight, he found that she also had been born on the Eastern Shore; they shared many memories. He did most of the talking, which was agreeable to both of them.

Frederick held Bible literacy classes on his free nights; he was consumed with a desire to help his people, slave and free, to read. When he realized that Anna could neither read nor write, he offered his services eagerly.

"Anna, I would count it a privilege to teach you to read God's Holy Word," said Frederick.

"But I'm not a preacher," said Anna. "And Mrs. Wells keeps me busy most nights." She smiled her haunting, tranquil smile. "Maybe it's better you tell me all about the Bible, 'cause you know so much."

Enchanted, Frederick munched another fragrant cinnamon bun and launched into a discourse on Exodus. Anna could not listen enough, it seemed. She also presented him with violin books, and she enjoyed playing audience even when he struggled with the difficult passages.

Frederick could hardly believe the best summer of his life was about to draw to a close.

"Frederick, are you coming with us to camp meeting next Saturday night?"

Henry Rolles smiled at him. "I hear Anna is going."

Spiritual renewal was just what he needed, Frederick decided. So he took his small valise of clothing with him to work on Saturday, intending to stop at Hugh's to make his weekly payment before he left for camp meeting. But his work ran late, and Frederick had to decide whether to make the payment or go with his friends.

I will make the payment tomorrow evening when we return, thought Frederick. *One day will make little difference.*

The all-black camp meeting was even better than

Frederick had hoped. Scores of Christians sang God's praises in rich rhythms and harmonies, clapping their hands. The preachers were fiery and powerful. All were welcome to approach the altars to seek God. Frederick was deeply moved. Frustration and anger in his life over slavery melted into a pure resolve to be free. But it was a resolve full of hope and trust in his Savior, unencumbered by hatred or rage.

God has been so good, Frederick mused, *so good.* Not only had He blessed Frederick with spiritual renewal, He had given him wonderful friends and, best of all, someone to love. For that Sunday evening after the preaching, Anna had put her hand in his and agreed to marry him.

I don't know how we will marry or when. Frederick was determined to have a family that lived together, without separation at the whim of a master. *But soon. It must be soon.* He fairly floated back to his tent.

A small, nagging voice in Frederick's head pointed out that he was to have returned Sunday night to pay Hugh.

I'll leave first thing in the morning—after I say goodbye to Anna.

"You black rascal! I have a great mind to give you a severe whipping!" Hugh exploded. "How dare you go out of the city without my permission. I am your master!"

"Sir," said Frederick, "I did not know that it was any part of the bargain that I should ask you when or where I should go."

"Did not *know?*" Hugh smashed his mug into the fireplace as his wife and children fled.

If he tries to flog me, I will defend myself. Even if that makes him sell me down South, I will not permit him to treat me like an animal. Frederick put the money carefully on the kitchen table and faced Hugh, his brain cool and alert.

Hugh saw the glint in Frederick's eye and stormed to the other side of the room. The two glared at each other in silence. Finally, Hugh spoke.

"You scoundrel! You have done for yourself; you shall hire your time no longer. The next thing I shall hear of will be your running away. Bring home your tools and your clothes, at once. I'll teach you how to go off in this way."[3]

"Benjamin, go see if Frederick wants to eat with us."

"Ah, Ma, I did it yesterday, and he just yelled at me to leave him alone. He's lazy, Ma, staying up in his bed all the time."

"Well, we'll just see about that!" Sophia blazed up the stairs and rapped smartly on Frederick's door. "Frederick, come out of that room this instant and eat. You'll get sick if you don't eat, and I don't have time to take care of sick people around here." She pounded vigorously. "Frederick, you hear me?"

"Yes, I'm comin'," said a thick voice. Frederick stumbled down the stairs and eyed dinner with little interest.

Goodness, the boy looks terrible, thought Sophia. *He hasn't shaven, his eyes look bloodshot—are those the clothes he came home in? And Frederick is always so particular, so neat!*

Has he gone out looking for work at all? Has he really been lying around upstairs the past day or two? If so, I will let Hugh deal with him. It was his idea to bring Frederick back. Sophia's sixth baby would be born soon; thank heaven Tommy and Annie were old enough to help out, or she would never have lived through this pregnancy.

Frederick shoveled the chowder in, eating merely because it was required. Then he again went upstairs.

"Lazy Freddy," said Benjamin.

"Wazy Fweddy," echoed little Edward.

"Hush!" said their mother. *Let Hugh deal with Frederick,* she repeated to herself.

Hugh had left at dawn and worked late all week, but not so late that he did not notice Frederick's indolence. He casually inquired of his wife at the beginning of the week about Frederick's activities. She answered that she had not noticed where he had gone; he seemed to keep to himself a great deal. His queries grew less patient. Sophia remained vague and unconcerned.

"Where is the money?" he demanded of Frederick after supper Saturday evening.

"Money?" Frederick answered with a puzzled air. "I am a slave, and have none, sir."

"The money! The money you are to give me every Saturday!" roared Hugh.

"When you ordered me back to your house, you gave me no other instruction," said Frederick. "I awaited your command."

Hugh swore, using epithets that even Frederick had never heard, even on the docks, and threatened to whip Frederick within an inch of his life. He watched carefully. Hugh was a dangerous, bearlike man when angry, and resisting him would be more difficult than fighting Covey. Suddenly, however, Hugh calmed himself.

"You need no longer bother yourself about finding work," he said softly, with a strange smile. "I will see to your work. Be assured you will have plenty." He turned on his heel and left the room.

Frederick spent most of Sunday in his room, thinking.

Hugh's sudden change unnerved him more than anything he had ever done. Hugh did not comment on his going to church; Hugh always had a few sarcastic remarks ready on Sunday mornings. Hugh had been civil during Sunday dinner, even urging Frederick to take more chicken so that he would be strong for his work.

Work? What work? Did Hugh mean that he would influence Thomas to sell him down South?

Frederick shivered. *I've been a fool,* he thought. *He has absolute power over me; what did I think I would accomplish by angering him? If Captain Auld hears about the camp meeting, he will believe Hugh.* Frederick weighed alternatives and prayed. His resolve once more became crystal-clear.

I must escape, and I must do it soon.

nine

F rederick?" Sophia Auld paused, her kettle steaming in her hand.

"Morning, Miss Sophia," said Frederick. His smooth, clean face broke into a smile, and he took the heavy kettle for his mistress. Frederick downed a quick breakfast of cold cornbread and headed out the door before Hugh even came down.

"Get out of bed," growled Hugh as he pounded on Frederick's door.

"Hush, you'll wake the little ones," remonstrated Sophia. "The boy has already gone to look for work."

"Indeed," said Hugh with the strange smile once more.

"Indeed," said Sophia firmly. She did not like the change in Hugh any more than Frederick did. They said no more.

Each morning Frederick left before dawn to work at Butler's shipyard, where he often served as foreman, despite his youth, and earned nine dollars per week. He brought his wages to Hugh each Saturday, and his master mellowed so much that he gave Frederick twenty-five cents.

"Put it to good use," Hugh said airily.

I will. I will use it to escape.

"Here it is, Frederick."

That was all Anna said, but tears welled up in his eyes. Anna had sold her two featherbeds, her most prized possessions. She put the small money bag in his hand.

"Anna—" His voice failed him.

"Don't, Frederick." Anna touched his lips gently.

Frederick had managed to save seventeen dollars that summer, not nearly enough to pay for his railroad fare North. Now that his wages went to Hugh, there was no chance for him to save more.

He would soon be sold down South. Frederick knew it in his bones.

He hated to leave Baltimore. He enjoyed his work. Frederick often clashed with Miss Sophia, but she was all the mother he had. He would miss his dear friends from the Mental Improvement Society.

And Anna—if he were captured in his escape attempt, her sacrifices were all for nothing. He would never see her heart-catching smile again.

He crushed her to his chest. "Pray, Anna. Pray that the Good God will help me escape, as He did the slaves in Egypt."

"I do, Frederick. I do."

Where is he?

Frederick tried not to let panic swell his throat shut. He sauntered around the train station, careful not to search for Isaac Rolles, who was to meet him at the last moment with his small baggage. Traveling blacks were often stopped and questioned by authorities, so Frederick had planned this

109

step in his escape. His train was pulling into the station, and he wanted to pick his seat carefully. *Where is Isaac? Why did I dare plan such folly? Perhaps God really does want black people to remain unthinking cattle.*

"God be with ye, Fred," said a voice beside him.

Before Frederick could say anything, the speaker was gone, and Frederick found himself on the platform carrying his satchel, casually entering the train to Wilmington as if he did it every day. He avoided buying his tickets at the station, afraid of being questioned. Instead, he chose to buy them directly from the conductor, which was a common practice. Frederick had seen a few acquaintances standing in line on other platforms. He needed to seat himself as quickly as possible.

Please don't let them sit in my car, Lord.

He found a seat in the last black car across from an old couple who were already napping. Given his exceptional height, unforgettable features, and golden skin, Frederick realized that traveling incognito simply would not work. So he chose to make use of his dramatic talents and shipyard background. A red shirt, tarpaulin hat, and black cravat tied carelessly completed his sailor's uniform. He sang a sea chantey and joked with the men around him, easily using the sailor's lingo that he knew well. The countryside flew past his window. Frederick was fascinated, as he had never ridden a train before. He wanted to stare! But he must convince those around him that he was a world traveler.

"Papers," said the conductor curtly. He scanned the freedman's papers of the couple nearest the door, then the two elderly women next to them.

Frederick held his breath. An older black freedman, a sailor, had loaned Frederick his precious sailor's protection papers, at the risk of losing his own freedom. They were not full freedman's papers, and Frederick looked nothing like the written description of his friend, who was older, shorter, and darker. But they were the best he could do.

Oh, Lord, make seeing eyes blind.

The conductor stood in front of Frederick, who smiled confidently, but did not immediately produce his papers, as the others had. The man relaxed visibly; he somehow found this reassuring.

"I suppose you have your free papers?" he asked.

"No, sir, I never carry my free papers at sea with me," declared Frederick.

"But you have something to indicate you are a free man, have you not?"

"Yes, sir," answered Frederick fervently. The entire car turned to listen to the dramatic tones of the gallant sailor. "I have a paper with the American eagle on it that will carry me round the world!"[1]

Scattered applause greeted Frederick's response. The United States and Great Britain were currently at odds over Britain's practice of searching American ships. Patriotism was at a fever pitch, with Americans often buying their sailors drinks and proclaiming them heroes. The conductor barely glanced at Frederick's papers, and all but saluted him. Frederick bought his ticket. The conductor finished checking other travelers' documents and left the car.

Frederick was glad when the travelers settled into drowsy boredom. He tried not to pant with relief. They were still in Maryland; some of his acquaintances who initially missed him in his sailor's outfit might eventually recognize him and report him to the conductor. But at least he had made it past this first obstacle.

Frederick had never traveled so fast in his life, but the train's speed seemed snail-like. Soon they would arrive at the ferry at Havre de Grace; Frederick would cross the Susquehanna River there, and continue on through Delaware. At Wilmington, he would take a steamship on the Delaware River to Philadelphia, if all went well.

If.

The conductor finally announced the train's arrival at Havre de Grace. Frederick disembarked, paid his passage, then stepped onto the ferry boat. The fresh breeze felt good after the crowded train, with its stifling odors of tobacco, food, and diapers.

"Halloo, Fred!"

Frederick stood like a statue.

"How are you, Fred? How's Baltimore? Where are you headed?" The deckhand, who had once worked along the wharves near Gardiner's shipyard, was glad to see his old acquaintance.

"Very fine, thank you. Have you worked here long?" asked Frederick quietly, hoping that Nichols would match his tone.

"Two months. Say, why in thunder are you dressed like a sailor? How could you enlist?"

"Hope Lizzie and the children are well," said Frederick desperately, and managed to separate himself from Nichols in the crowd. He made his way quickly to a throng on the opposite side of the boat and prayed that Nichols would not find him. When the ferry finally bumped on the opposite shore, Frederick resisted the temptation to leap over the rails, and tagged along with a group of swarthy workmen on their way to Philadelphia.

Frederick found a seat on the train opposite two women. The view out his window froze his blood. Seated in a stationary southbound train was Captain McGowan, whose ship Frederick had caulked at Price's shipyard only a few

days before! Captain McGowan had personally congratu-
lated him on his excellent work. The trains were so close
that Frederick could read the headlines on his newspaper.

Oh, Lord, I'm dead.

But Captain McGowan seemed a bit distraught; he kept
checking under his seat.

Frederick remained motionless, unable to stir.

His train lurched forward.

He had made it this far, but Wilmington was ahead—
Wilmington, at the edge of Delaware, the last slave state
before the free North. Slave hunters watched the Delaware
border day and night.

*Almighty God, do You truly make men slaves and expect
them to live as animals? I cannot believe it. Help me, help
me, Father of all men.*

"Where can I get a train to New York?" Frederick spoke the
fantastic words as calmly as if he had asked directions to a
new job in Baltimore.

A German blacksmith had eyed him on the train after
the McGowan incident; Frederick knew him well. But the
man said nothing, and evidently decided not to report him.
When the train passengers disembarked for the steamship at
Wilmington, Frederick felt his heart pound so, it seemed
that his red shirt must rise and fall so everyone could see it.
Any moment a slave hunter would grab his arms, throw him
to the ground, lock on the chains.

*You—the big yella-skinned one. How'd you like me for
your new master?*

But nothing had happened.

Nothing.

The big steamer chugged away on the sparkling Delaware River. Frederick rode numbly. When the boat docked,

Frederick followed the other passengers mechanically.

He carried his valise into the busy afternoon traffic that was Philadelphia.

Free Philadelphia.

Frederick tried to feel elation. He thanked God for His mercy and providence.

But he could feel nothing.

He must go to New York.

"Thank you, sir," Frederick said, and followed the man's directions to the Willow Street station. He rode the train once more, arriving about one o'clock in the morning.

Today, September 4, 1838, said Frederick to himself as he hauled his valise down the deserted city street, *you are free.*

Frederick stirred uneasily; why were his feet so cold, his back stiff? Had he been sent back to Covey's, where he often slept in the barn? Frederick opened his eyes warily.

But his fears turned to overwhelming joy as he realized that the alley where he had slept, pillowing his head on his valise, was in New York.

"Caanan land, sweet Caanan land!" Frederick sang. He laughed at the sunshine, laughed at the dirty, crooked streets, laughed at the men who drove irritably past the black man who appeared to have continued his previous night's drinking binge.

I've been rescued from the lions' den. Those lions didn't get me, no, siree!

All day long Frederick celebrated. *Thank You, Lord. Thank You, Lord.* He could not breathe enough of the sweet, free air.

"I lived more in one day than in a year of my slave life," wrote Frederick later. "It was a time of joyous excitement which words can but tamely describe."[2] Frederick simply walked the first two days of his freedom. Liberty to turn right when one wished! Liberty to turn left!

But eventually the intoxication wore off, and Frederick became aware that he was not only free from slavery, but also "free from food and shelter as well."[3] His tiny store of money ran out.

He also found that New York was not nearly as hospitable as he had hoped. In wandering the streets, he encountered another escaped slave that he had known in Maryland as Dr. Allender's Jake. He was overjoyed to see a familiar face, but Jake was not the easygoing man he remembered. He had narrowly escaped recapture. "Stay away from the docks," he warned Frederick. "Don't go to any of the colored boardinghouses. Slave hunters watch them all. They have spies everywhere." He could not even trust fellow blacks, as some were willing to pass information about runaways for a price.

Jake looked about him fearfully, then suddenly walked away in the opposite direction.

I do believe he thinks I am a spy, thought Frederick, his heart sinking. He had hoped for a helping hand, someone to point him in the right direction. New York suddenly seemed lonely and dangerous.

I can't work at the wharves. That is the first place Thomas or Hugh would look. I know no one. Frederick jammed his hands into his empty pockets. The light was rapidly fading, and he needed somewhere to spend the night, as it looked as if it might rain. Perhaps the docks might not be so perilous in the evening as they were in broad daylight. Frederick headed towards the sea and searched along the wharves until he found a large, empty barrel.

Not a palace, but it will do. He crawled into it headfirst.

His feet and knees, protruding from the end, felt the first cold raindrops of the stormy night.

"Good evening, sir," said Frederick, forcing a smile to his lips. He hated begging, but he could not remember the last time he had eaten. "Would you care to help a poor traveler?"

The bent, grizzled old sailor looked at Frederick with a keen pair of black eyes. "Hungry, young man?" he asked. "Come home with me, and I'll see what's in the pot."

Frederick felt as if he would collapse from relief. He was too ravenous to worry about slave hunters. The old man led him to the door of a little shack.

"My name is Stuart," said his benefactor. He ladled beans into a large, cracked bowl and placed them in front of Frederick, who had never smelled anything quite so good.

"Thanks be to God," said Frederick, and with the brief prayer, gobbled the meal down.

"Have some more," said Stuart. "You're still a growin' one, aren't ya? Need plenty of grub to put on those tall bones. It's chilly for this time of year, and close to dark. You stay here tonight, and tomorrow we see what we can do."

"You are God's angel, sir," said Frederick. The old man put a little more coal on the fire and pointed to an old bed in the corner.

"Good night, boy," said Stuart.

In Stuart's mouth, "boy" is no insult, thought Frederick, as he pulled the ragged blanket to his chin. He felt that he was at Uncle Lawson's once more.

"Not that you would need to know," said Stuart, "but I know some gentlemen who help many poor travelers." Again, his sharp eyes appraised Frederick. *Can he see my very bones?* Frederick wondered.

"I would greatly appreciate their assistance," said Frederick, sipping his hot coffee with satisfaction.

Stuart and Frederick walked to the corner of Lispenard and Church Streets. *It is good to have a friend,* thought Frederick. *God made human beings to dwell together.*

The two circled the block behind a large house with an ornate door. Stuart went to the back and knocked. A maid whisked them into a small side room, and a few minutes later a pleasant-looking gentleman held his hand out to Frederick.

"My pleasure, Mr.—"

"Johnson, sir."

"Mr. Johnson, my wife and I would be more than happy to have you as our guest until you can make other arrangements." David Ruggles, the leader of the New York City underground railroad, smiled. "I know you wish to return certain papers to a gentleman back in Maryland. I also understand that a young lady awaits news of your arrival here."

"Oh, yes, sir!" Frederick could not suppress his eagerness. "I wish to get a message to Miss Anna Murray as soon as possible."

"We will help you with both letters. Of course, we will send them from different addresses. Meanwhile, you must rest from your travels. I understand that it has been a difficult journey."

"Yes, sir."

"Mary will show you to your room. Do you read, sir?"

"Oh, yes!" answered Frederick. He had brought only Uncle Lawson's Bible in his valise.

"We have a fairly large library; it would not be advisable to frequent it during the day, but perhaps tonight you might find something of interest."

Am I in heaven, Lord? To browse in a whole roomful of books was an unthinkable privilege. Frederick's eyes filled with tears.

"Thank you, Mr. Ruggles," he said incoherently. "Thank you, Stuart. God bless you."

"I, Anna, take thee, Frederick, to be my lawfully wedded husband."

Anna calmly repeated her wedding vows in the Ruggleses' back parlor. Frederick watched the September sun polish her walnut skin, glisten in her black hair and fathomless eyes. Her hand in his was warm and sure, as they stood before Rev. J. W. C. Pennington. The prominent Presbyterian minister, himself a former runaway slave, had agreed to waive his marriage fee.

It is not a dream. We will soon be man and wife.

How he had longed for this moment! All his life he had craved someone to love, someone who would love him. Slavery had snatched him from life with his mother, stolen him from Grandmammy Bailey. Slavery ruined his relationships with Miss Lucretia and Miss Sophia. Frederick had shrunk from the casual bonds many young slave men and women forged, knowing any moment they could be parted from each other and their children. Something deep within him cried out for a woman who would listen, laugh, and work with him for a lifetime.

These vows are no guarantee, said a cold voice in Frederick's mind. *Hugh or Thomas Auld can recapture you, sell you down South, and have Anna put in prison for consorting with a runaway—all nice and legal.*

Frederick shook the ugly threats off and smiled at his bride as she finished her pledge.

Someday, perhaps, our children will make these vows

without fear that man will put them asunder. Until then, I must look to God for help in my keeping them.

"I, Frederick, take thee, Anna, to be my lawfully wedded wife, to have and to hold from this day forward. . . ."

ten

O h, Frederick, a house of our own! Room for a garden right back here—we'll plant tomatoes and peas! It's so cold up here. Wonder when you start plantin'?"

Frederick grinned, enjoying his wife's delight. The tiny house at the end of Elm Street in Bedford, Massachusetts, was an answer to their prayers.

The day of their marriage, Frederick and Anna had said grateful good-byes to Rev. Pennington, the Ruggleses, and Stuart. It was dangerous, they agreed, for the newlyweds to remain in New York. Once united, they should leave immediately for Bedford, Massachusetts, which had a reputation of hospitality to runaway slaves, as many Quakers lived there. Frederick would also have more employment opportunities. So the new "Johnsons" rode the steamboat *John W. Richmond* to Newport, Rhode Island. Frederick was grateful for the Indian summer weather, as the black newlyweds were not permitted inside the cabins or in the dining rooms. After a chilly night spent on deck, the two disembarked and spotted a stagecoach with the yellow letters "New Bedford" emblazoned across it. Frederick found, to his dismay, that he did not have enough money to pay their fares. What would they do, stranded in Newport?

"Thee get in," said a quiet voice.

William Taber, a passenger simply yet richly dressed, motioned Frederick and Anna into the coach. He and Joseph Ricketson, another Quaker, smiled at the two. Reassured, they did so.

"Where's your money?" the driver asked Frederick during a breakfast stop, which Frederick and Anna ignored.

"You shall have it when we reach New Bedford," said Frederick impulsively.

To his surprise, the man did not protest. But he did retain their luggage when they arrived at their destination. All their worldly possessions, including a few clothes and Frederick's violin and precious music books, were in their valises.

"I'll give 'em to ya when you pay," said the driver.

Frederick thought this only fair, but had no idea what to do.

"Welcome, young folks," said Nathan Johnson. His black face shone with kindness. "How much do they need?"

"Two dollars," said the stagecoach driver.

Johnson loaned Frederick the money, and the relieved couple accompanied him to his home, where they met his wife, Mary, who ran a catering service.

Frederick and Anna soon sampled one of Mary's justifiably famous dinners, and finally retired to their own bedroom after spending the first two days of their marriage in crowded carriages and on cold ship decks. Anna enjoyed cooking with Mary in her huge kitchen. Frederick found that Nathan, to his amazement, was a member of the Taber

Library Society, the only black man in town who actually met with the many white wealthy businessmen. Nathan himself was quite prosperous. Frederick marveled at such a novelty.

In the South, non-slave owners were generally poverty-stricken and illiterate. To Frederick's surprise, the working class in New Bedford, both black and white, owned well-kept homes equipped with all sorts of inventions.

"Instead of going a hundred yards to the spring, the maid-servant had a well or pump at her elbow. . . . Here were sinks, drains, self-shutting gates, pounding-barrels, washing-machines, wringing machines, and a hundred other contrivances for saving time and money."[1]

He was impressed, too, with the industry and ingenuity of the men who worked at the wharves. "Everybody seemed in earnest. The carpenter struck the nail on its head, and the caulkers wasted no strength in idle flourishes of their mallets. Ships brought here for repairs were made stronger and better than when new."[2]

Work done by dozens of reluctant slaves in the South was managed by a few motivated workers in the free North.

Frederick was amazed to hear that black children often attended school with white children, but he was flabbergasted when Nathan told him that a black man, theoretically, could be elected governor of the state.

All this existed, all those years I was a slave, thought Frederick.

He was eager to work, and celebrated his first wages: two silver half-dollars given him by Mrs. Ephraim Peabody, the Unitarian minister's wife, for shoveling coal. He soon discovered that the whaling ships that made New Bedford a rich town needed a great deal of wood. He borrowed money from Nathan to buy a saw and buck, and asked the store clerk for a "fip's" worth of cord to brace his saw in the frame.

"You're not from around here!" growled the clerk. A fip was about six and a quarter cents in Maryland; no such currency existed in New Bedford.

Frederick's stomach knotted, and he left quickly with his purchases.

"You don't have anything to worry about," Nathan assured him. "People in New Bedford, black and white, don't like slave catchers. Once a black man talked about his intention to contact a slave owner about his runaway Sol, who worked on the docks here. That scoundrel went to a special meeting called by his church, the Third Christian Church. They had the usual prayers, elections, and procedures. Then the president of the congregation named the betrayer, and said, 'Well, friends and brethren, we have got him here, and I would recommend that you, young men, should take him outside the door and kill him!'[3] The man jumped through a window and was never seen in this town again!" Nathan laughed merrily.

"I would, however," Nathan advised, "change your last name. There are too many black Johnsons in this town!" He grinned. Nathan was reading Sir Walter Scott's "Lady of the Lake" and suggested that Frederick and Anna take the name of Douglas, after the poem's hero. Frederick saw the wisdom of this, and decided to spell his new name the way several distinguished families in Baltimore did. "Frederick Bailey" and "Frederick Johnson" disappeared.

Frederick was overjoyed when Rodney French, a white abolitionist, hired him to caulk a whaling ship for the excellent wages of two dollars a day. But he found that New Bedford was not the heaven that he originally envisioned. When Frederick showed up on his first day of work, the other caulkers, who were white, threatened to walk off their job. Disappointed but not surprised, he sawed wood, loaded coal, excavated cellars, cleaned yards, scrubbed ship decks, and hauled goods onto ships for one dollar per day. It was not much, but it enabled him to pay the Johnsons back and rent this tiny home.

He needed to make more money, however. Anna was expecting their first child. *Babies need lots of things,* mused Frederick proudly. *Our first child will be free.* His heart swelled with thanksgiving. *O Lord, You are so good.*

Frederick's reputation as a reliable worker grew, and he obtained better employment. He worked for several Quaker businessmen, including Joseph Ricketson, one of the men who had encouraged him and his new wife to "get in" the stagecoach bound for New Bedford. Ricketson owned a whaling oil refinery, where Frederick worked alongside whites and blacks. Frederick later worked at a foundry and on the docks repairing whaling ships.

Frederick loved coming home from a hard day's work to talk with Anna, eat her thrifty but succulent meals, and hold baby Rosetta on his lap. Memories of Rowena Auld's weekly half-peck of cornmeal, Covey's whippings, and Hugh's rages finally began to fade. He found himself often giving thanks for the simple pleasures of freedom, and yearning to grow close to the God he had angrily questioned during the worst times of his slavery.

But Frederick and Anna could not worship equally with whites, even in New Bedford. Frederick was excited when he found that the Elm Street Methodist Church was racially mixed, but disappointed when he was asked to sit in the gallery, to make room for the unconverted. He did so, not wanting to alienate any lost souls from the joy of the gospel. But when only church members attended a Communion service, he fully expected an open, friendly sharing of the sacred wine and bread. "Although they disowned, in effect, their black brothers and sisters before the world, I did think that where none but the saints were assembled, and no offense could be given to the wicked, and the gospel could not be 'blamed,' they would certainly recognize us as children of the same Father, and heirs of the same salvation, on equal terms with themselves."[4] Instead, the few black members who descended from the gallery to back seats were served last, while the pastor patronizingly told them that "God is no respecter of persons." While Frederick had to admit that no one had forced the black members to wait, he felt they were unwanted. Frederick and Anna left. To their dismay, they found the same atmosphere in all the churches in New Bedford. Even though Quakers considered slavery an abomination and were so politically active in their convictions, very few black members were present in their meetings.

So, the prejudice that so stains Your congregations in the South flourishes in those of the North, as well. Lord, is this why You died for men? Your Church is wicked! Wicked!

Frederick finally visited a small black congregation called Zion Methodists, who met in a schoolhouse on Second Street. They welcomed him, Anna, Rosetta, and little Lewis Henry, with open arms. The love and respect they gave the Douglass family healed some of the anger Frederick experienced towards much of the white Christian community. Frederick served as sexton, steward, class leader, clerk, and lay preacher. His new pastor, Thomas James, a former runaway slave who thoroughly integrated his activism against slavery with his strong Christian faith, encouraged and supported his intelligent, gifted parishioner.

One evening at a community church meeting in which

racial topics were discussed, Rev. James asked Frederick to speak. Frederick passionately discredited black colonization, a popular plan in which blacks would be sent back to Africa to live. Some thought this would eliminate the racial problem in the United States.

"Why should I be deported as if I had committed a crime?" asked Frederick. "This country is my home. I am an American. The only crime committed—slavery—was committed *against* me." He went on to describe his personal experience as a slave. His listeners included many white abolitionists. Frederick was astonished to find that the *Liberator,* a newspaper owned and edited by William Lloyd Garrison, later mentioned his speech. When Frederick had been free only a few months, a young black man had approached him to subscribe to this paper. Frederick declined, saying he was a poor runaway slave, and could not afford the small fee. The young man had given him a free subscription, and Frederick had become a fervent follower of Garrison, who believed that the Bible taught that Christians, black or white, were part of one body with Jesus Christ as its head. "It [the paper] detested slavery and made no truce with the traffickers in the bodies and souls of men. It preached human brotherhood; it exposed hypocrisy and wickedness in high places; it denounced oppression and with all the solemnity of 'Thus saith the Lord,' demanded the complete emancipation of my race. I loved this paper and its editor," Frederick wrote later.[5] He later heard Garrison speak against slavery; surprised by his unassuming appearance, Frederick was amazed at the vehemence in the voice of William Lloyd Garrison. "Prejudice against color is rebellion against God!" he thundered.[6]

"A white man," marveled Frederick one evening to Anna

126

over dinner. "A white man feels this way about slavery."

She smiled; it was good to see him so inspired. He had been moody and irritable as they visited church after church, feeling rejected. Anna was content to have plenty for her family to eat, a pleasant, clean little home, and the freedom that New Bedford did offer. Frederick, Anna sighed as she cleared the dishes, always seemed to need more.

He continued to attend abolitionist meetings in the area, drinking in the strong opposition to slavery by both whites and blacks, occasionally speaking up. But "it was enough for me to listen, to receive, and applaud the great words of others and only whisper in private, among the white laborers on the wharves and elsewhere, the truths which burned in my heart."[7]

But in the summer of 1841, Frederick's quiet personal revolution emerged as one that would change the world forever.

eleven

M r. Douglass! How glad I am to see thee at this meeting!"

Frederick stammered a polite response. He had no idea that William C. Coffin, a well-off white Quaker businessman, had heard him speak at an antislavery meeting in New Bedford. Oblivious to the racially separate customs that pervaded even antislavery meetings, Coffin took his arm and walked with Frederick as if they were good friends.

"Would you be willing, sir, to speak at this meeting should the Spirit so move you?"

Frederick stared, speechless. He had come to Nantucket, an abolitionist stronghold, to hear some of the most prominent speakers of his day. He had no idea anyone would want him to address the whole Massachusetts Anti-Slavery Society.

"Y–yes, if you wish," he answered weakly.

"Good! I will inform Mr. Collins, and we will hope to hear from you."

That hot August evening Coffin and several of his friends escorted Frederick to the meeting at the Big Shop, an enormous building in which whaling ships were often constructed. The Society had reserved the ornate Nantucket cultural center for the event, but when the town fathers heard that blacks, including a black speaker, were invited, they canceled their permit for the lovely auditorium. So people gathered by the hundreds at the Big Shop; when it filled, they stood at the windows and even climbed to the rafters. Swinging their legs, they listened to William Lloyd Garrison decry the racial prejudice in the North. Burly, resolute Quaker men quietly wandered the perimeters, on the lookout for troublemakers. Local abolitionists spoke at length. Some listeners became restless as the hour grew late. Finally, Frederick rose from his seat.

His mouth felt as if he eaten a chicken, feathers and all. He could not get enough air. Thousands of people—mostly white—stared at him. On every side sat famous men whom he idolized: Garrison, of course, as well as Wendell Phillips, Parker Pillsbury, Edmund Quincy, and John A. Collins, the head of the Massachusetts Anti-Slavery Society. Lucretia Coffin Mott, a defender of blacks and an early women's rights advocate, smiled encouragingly at him, but Frederick's mind was a vacuum. He must say *something*.

"I—I do apologize for my slowness of speech, ladies and gentlemen," Frederick stuttered. *Think. Think. I must help them know what slavery was like.* Later Frederick regretted that he could remember almost nothing of his first major speech other than the terror of it. But the effect it had on William Lloyd Garrison changed the jittery crowd into a multitude of ardent abolitionists.

"Have we been listening to a thing, a chattel personal, or a man?" he asked.

129

"A man! A man!" the audience shouted with one accord.

"Shall such a man be held a slave in a Christian land?" called out Garrison.

Anna Gardner, who was to be Douglass's loyal friend for the rest of their long lives, remembered the whole scene: " 'No! No!' shouted the audience. Raising his voice to its fullest note, he again asked, 'Shall such a man ever be sent back to bondage from the free soil of old Massachusetts?' With a tremendous roar the whole assembly sprang to its feet and continued shouting, 'No! No! No!' " Garrison's voice was lost in their vehemence.[1]

Frederick stood with them, his distinguished colleagues clapping him on the back and applauding.

"Mr. Douglass, would you honor our Society by serving as an agent for us? You can see what a powerful effect your speech had on the meeting tonight. Surely you would wish to strike a strong blow against slavery!"

"I certainly would, Mr. Collins," Frederick answered slowly. *How can this be happening?* he thought incredulously. *To be paid to discredit the evils of slavery?* "But I have only been free three years. I have had no schooling, sir," Frederick told him. "And I fear that if I make such public statements, my old master will find me."

"You are a graduate from a most peculiar institution, with your diploma written on your back," said Collins.[2] "None of us has felt your stripes, although we deeply sympathize with your race. No one, sir, can tell your story as you do. We, your friends, shall not leave you, day or night. Your old master shall never lay hands on you, never."

Frederick reluctantly agreed to think about Collins's proposal, then went back to New Bedford to work at a shipyard and ponder the opportunity before him.

"I will agree to three months of speaking engage-
ments," he finally told Anna one night after Rosetta and
Lewis Henry were asleep. "Three months only. Perhaps
then they will realize that I am no black William Lloyd
Garrison, and will leave me in peace. The salary will help
keep you and the children." He held her close.

Anna said little. Mrs. Wilson and Mrs. Tolliver had
praised her mending, and wanted several dresses made. The
salary Frederick had mentioned sounded good, but Anna
could see no guarantees as to when and how the money
would reach her. She herself would make sure that the children wanted for nothing while Frederick was gone. It was
too soon to tell him of the new little one; Anna would wait
until his return to give him the news. She hugged Frederick
and made herself smile.

The gentleness of it broke his heart. "Soon, my love. I'll
be home soon."

"My whole heart went with the holy cause, and my most
fervent prayer to the Almighty Disposer of the hearts of
men was continually offered for its early triumph. In this
enthusiastic spirit I dropped into the ranks of freedom's
friends and went forth to the battle," wrote Frederick.[3]
Frederick missed his family, but found travel exciting, his
companions stimulating, his audiences attentive. Every
night Frederick spoke in churches, meetinghouses, town
halls, and auditoriums, telling about plantation life, Old
Master and Esther, and Thomas Auld's refusal to save him
from the villainous Covey. The sentences that had clogged
his soul poured out so eloquently that Frederick astonished
himself, as well as his friends. Word of his articulate testi-
monial against slavery spread from town to town. Collins,
Garrison, and other abolitionist leaders recognized that the

Massachusetts Anti-Slavery Society had a new weapon! At the end of the three months, they asked Frederick to accept a permanent position as a lecturer.

"Why would you humiliate yourself so before those white people?" questioned Alphonso Davis, who had befriended Frederick since his early days in New Bedford. "We who have escaped slavery never want to think of it again. I hear they even want you to take off your shirt so they can see the scars where Covey whipped you."

Embarrassed, Frederick tried to explain to his friend. "I am not proud of slavery; I wish to destroy it! Even if I must debase myself, I will do so to fight the evil."

The Society pleaded with Frederick; his New Bedford friends, black and white, debated with him. But Anna, now obviously pregnant with their third child, said little.

"I must do this, Anna, I must. If we defeat slavery, then black children will no longer grow up in fear of the lash. God Himself wants to rescue them!"

"Try to come home before the baby is born," said Anna, her lower lip trembling a little.

Frederick held her hand in both of his.

Frederick scanned the stack of handwritten pages before him critically. Conscious of his lack of formal education, he wanted his *Narrative of the Life of Frederick Douglass, an American Slave,* to be perfect before he gave it to his friend Wendell Phillips to evaluate.

I wrote a book. I, myself! Frederick could not suppress a surge of wicked delight. *Hugh and Sophia Auld would not permit me to learn to read, but I have written a book!*

Would Phillips consider it worthy of publication? What would his other Anti-Slavery Society friends say about the *Narrative*? Frederick marveled for the hundredth time that these white men had grown so close to him. They had traveled hundreds of miles together as advocates for the cause of freedom.

I cannot believe it has been four years since I began speaking for the Society. I was so overjoyed at the prospect of striking a blow for liberty! Frederick grinned ruefully. *I even felt guilty about receiving a salary and wished I could suffer for the cause as the early proponents had.*

He need not have worried. New England, home of the most passionate abolitionists in the land, was still a stronghold of racial prejudice.

Frederick first accompanied Stephen S. Foster, Parker Pillsbury, Abby Kelley, and James Monroe to a convention in Rhode Island, where they presented the radical idea that the state should grant the vote to all men. Even Abby, the beautiful young Quakeress, was pelted with rotten eggs. Undaunted, the delegation traveled throughout Rhode Island to plead their cause before the people.

Frederick was routinely ejected from train cars when he tried to ride with his white friends. He spent many nights on steamboat decks, as only whites were allowed to have cabins. James Monroe often slept between cotton bales with Frederick on those cold, damp nights. Wendell Phillips refused to ride first class on a train when his friend was banished to a dirty Jim Crow car. J. N. Buffum, a lifelong friend of Frederick's, protested vigorously to Superintendent Stephen A. Chase of the Eastern Railroad when Frederick was dragged from a first-class car by six brawny train workers: "You often allowed dogs and monkeys to ride in first class cars, yet excluded a man like Frederick Douglass!"[4] Other abolitionist friends walked out of restaurants when the owners balked at serving Frederick. Grateful for their support, Frederick tried to dissuade them: "When traveling in company with my white friends I always urged them to leave me and go into the cabin and take their comfortable berths. I saw no reason why they should be miserable because I was. Some of them took my advice very readily. I confess, however, that while I was entirely honest in urging them to go, and saw no principle that should bind them to stay and suffer with me, I always felt a little nearer to those who did not take my advice and persisted in sharing my hardships with me."[5]

When the young slavery fighters found they were not welcome in hotels, abolitionist families often invited the them to stay. Frederick not only appreciated his hosts' hospitality, but their help in educating him in proper manners. As a result, Frederick felt more at ease as he traveled.

Most towns had at least one church or room where Frederick and his friends were allowed to speak. When they were refused, the antislavery speakers made their speeches out in the open, usually in front of the church that had refused them.

Once Frederick, alone, tried to reserve a hall in which to speak in Grafton, Connecticut. No one, it seemed, wanted to hear the young black abolitionist. Defiantly, Frederick borrowed a dinner bell from a sympathetic hotel owner, and strode up and down the main streets of Grafton, proclaiming, "NOTICE! Frederick Douglass, a former slave, will speak on American slavery, on Grafton Common, this evening at seven o'clock. Those who would like to hear the truth about slavery from one of the slaves are respectfully invited to attend!" Amazed by the striking, golden-skinned man with the resonant baritone voice, the townspeople crowded the square that evening to hear Frederick. A pastor in the audience agreed to open his church for meetings, and Grafton's abolitionist movement grew by leaps and bounds.

In 1843 the Massachusetts Anti-Slavery Society, now part of the American Anti-Slavery Society, increased its vision: one hundred conventions were to be held in the Midwest, as well as New England.

Six months. What an ordeal it was! Frederick shook his head as he remembered the group's frequently cold receptions, even in places like Syracuse, New York, where the abolitionist movement, led by Gerrit Smith, had already flourished.

Frederick glanced at his right hand. It was much better, but had healed crookedly after a mob attacked Frederick and the others in Pendleton, Indiana. They had begun meetings in the local Baptist church, but were asked to stop because the church fathers feared that hecklers would destroy the church. Abolitionist sympathizers built a large platform in a nearby woods where a large crowd gathered. They were not going to quit! Frederick felt the thrill of satisfaction he always did when he and his coworkers managed to penetrate difficult territory.

I should have realized they would not quit, either, Frederick thought with regret. *I saw their eyes. I should have seen it coming.*

"Silence!" a grizzled man had shouted when William A. White began his first speech.

"We must speak, sir," said White. "The message we have is of utmost importance and one the Almighty Himself would have you hear."

"If you don't shut your fancy, lyin' mouth, you'll regret it," said another. A murmur of angry assent ran through the audience. Frederick saw more men emerge, two by two from the woods.

"Nevertheless, sir," said White firmly, "it is our right to address this group."

A shower of rotten eggs and stones hit the makeshift stage. But none of the rocks did any damage, and Frederick, White, and George Bradburn all held their ground, unperturbed, stinking eggs dripping from their faces. The angry mob members were at a loss. Where was the cringing terror they expected?

Bradburn spoke calmly, listing the evils of slavery and presenting reasons for the need for its abolition. A man in the crowd, named James Jackson, shouted that if he was up there, he could give a hundred reasons why the blacks should stay in their place.

"Please, sir, we would be happy to debate with you," said White, a Harvard graduate. "Feel free to join us."

Jackson mounted the stage with bravado and much applause from the mob. He was no match, however, for the brilliant White; he swore continually and threatened his opponents. One of his friends, tired of the embarrassing spectacle, climbed onto the stage and began ripping the makeshift pulpit apart. Dozens of enraged listeners mobbed the platform, shredding it and knocking William White senseless to the ground, his head bleeding profusely. Frederick grabbed a large cudgel and fought his attackers, only to be flattened himself.

"He struck a white man! KILL THE NIGGER!"

When Frederick awoke to a cloud of pain, a plain farmer's face met his tortured eyes.

"Don't move, Mr. Douglass. We will soon have thee and Mr. White to a safe place."

"Where are they?" asked Frederick, grasping frantically for his club.

"All gone home—most of them back to Andersonville," answered the farmer. His mild eyes narrowed. "Pack of cowards," he muttered under his breath. "Thee will be safe with us, Mr. Douglass."

Frederick lay back in the wagon, thanking God for his deliverer. The Quaker farmer, Neal Hardy, drove the injured men to his home, where his wife greeted them with horror and concern. Frederick and William found themselves bathed and resting in soft featherbeds. Two days later both mounted a platform in Noblesville, Indiana, to speak once more against slavery.

Neither would ever forget their kind hostess and her compassionate care.

Mrs. Hardy's soup tasted just like Anna's, remembered Frederick. *It was as if God had sent an angel to bind our wounds and give us food from heaven. But it made me miss Anna and the children even more.*

Frederick's frequent absences had been hard on his family. He had made it home when both Frederick and Charles Remond, named after his good friend and fellow black orator, were born. His children delighted him; he enjoyed their beautiful, well-fed little bodies and bright, inquisitive eyes. Rosetta was already interested in books, and her father taught her the alphabet and read to her and her small brothers by the hour when he was home.

Anna is such a good mother, Frederick mused gratefully. *She is an excellent household manager, even though she cannot read or write. And she is a good wife, always welcoming me when I come in, drained from my endeavors for the cause.* Frederick felt a pang of uneasiness. Anna rarely protested anymore when he left on another journey. Sometimes he wondered if she had adjusted too well to his absences. . . .

Now that the Society wants me home to work on my Narrative, *perhaps we can spend more time together. Anna loves music; maybe we can attend a concert in the park this*

Sunday afternoon, Frederick thought. *But right now, I must finish editing this manuscript so that Wendell can give me his opinion of it! The language of that last page was not quite right. . . .*

"Mr. Douglass! We applaud your courage, your devotion to the cause of freedom. But, sir, do you not think that your condemnation of religion is an affront to Him who died for us all?"

The earnest white clergyman at the New Bedford community meeting awaited Frederick's reply. Skirts, fans, and boots rustled loudly; what would the now-famous hometown radical say to this prosperous, comfortable audience that met to discuss cultural affairs?

Frederick eyed his listeners unflinchingly, and began. "What I have said respecting and against religion, I mean strictly to apply to the *slaveholding religion* of this land, and with no possible reference to Christianity proper; for, between the Christianity of this land, and the Christianity of Christ, I recognize the widest possible difference—so wide that to receive the one as good, pure, and holy, is of necessity to reject the other as bad, corrupt, and wicked."[6]

"I love the religion of our blessed Savior. I love that religion that comes from above, in the 'wisdom of God, which is first pure, then peaceable, gentle, and easy to be entreated, full of mercy and good fruits, without partiality, and without hypocrisy.' I love that religion that sends its votaries to bind up the wounds of him that has fallen among thieves. I love that religion that makes it the duty of its disciples to visit the fatherless and the widow in their affliction. I love that religion that is based upon the glorious principle of love to God and love to man; which makes its followers do unto others as they themselves would be done by. . . . It is because I

138

love this religion that I hate the slaveholding, the woman-whipping, the mind-darkening, the soul-destroying religion that exists in the southern states of America.[7]

"I am filled with unutterable loathing when I contemplate the religious pomp and show, together with the horrible inconsistencies, which everywhere surround me. We have men-stealers for ministers, women-whippers for missionaries, and cradle-plunderers for church members. The man who wields the blood-clotted cowskin during the week fills the pulpit on Sunday, and claims to be a minister of the meek and lowly Jesus. The man who robs me of my earnings at the end of each week meets me as a class-leader on Sunday morning, to show me the way of life, and the path of salvation. He who sells my sister, for purposes of prostitution, stands forth as the pious advocate of purity. He who proclaims it a religious duty to read the Bible denies me the right of learning to read the name of the God who made me. He who is the religious advocate of marriage robs whole millions of its sacred influence, and leaves them to the ravages of wholesale pollution.[8]

"They love the heathen on the other side of the globe. They can pray for him, pay money to have the Bible put into his hand, and missionaries to instruct him; while they despise and totally neglect the heathen at their own doors. . . .

" 'Shall I not visit for these things?' saith the Lord. 'Shall not my soul be avenged on such a nation as this?' "[9]

A crash of applause exploded the room after a moment's dead silence. The clergyman who had asked Frederick the question clapped frantically, but Frederick saw others sitting woodenly in their pews, their faces blank with hatred.

"Frederick, your *Narrative* is a masterful work! No wonder

your opponents claim you were never a slave! Your language and expression are very good. But if I were you, sir, I would burn that book to ashes!"

Frederick stared at Wendell Phillips in confusion, then nodded.

"The Aulds will find me," he said simply.

"I fear they will. Even though you give no details of your escape in the book, you may be sure they will guess your identity and send slave hunters to pursue you. The story must be told. But if it is published, you must never, *never* travel alone again, especially near the Southern states. You might think of leaving the country until the tempest is over."

"Surely such a small book will not make such a stir," protested Frederick.

"It surely will. I believe the Society must watch this situation closely. We must never underestimate the evil in some men's hearts."

twelve

Frederick watched the Atlantic swell into hypnotic green walls of water, then disintegrate with a roar, lifting the large ship *Cambria* as if it were a twig. Soon he and his friend James Buffum would arrive in England. England! In all his wildest dreams, Frederick had never envisioned such a journey. But the Anti-Slavery Society agreed with Phillips's assessment of possible response to his *Narrative of the Life of Frederick Douglass.* He must be overseas before the full impact of the book struck.

The Society also wanted to strengthen ties with its British counterparts. Abolitionists in Great Britain had successfully pushed for the end of slavery in the West Indies. Their organization, flushed with victory, was eager to support similar success in the United States. What better ambassador to send from America than a man who had once been a slave?

This has been an amazing voyage, Frederick thought. It began as many of his travels had: with controversy. The ship's steward refused Frederick the first-class cabin for which he had paid and banished him to steerage. A day or two into the voyage, however, the stringent racial rules that were enforced in the United States were relaxed considerably. Frederick found himself welcome even in the dining room. The captain asked his famous passenger to lecture on slavery, and Frederick spoke to an audience that included outraged tourists from New Orleans and Georgia.

"Throw him overboard! He shall not insult the gentle South!" the aristocratic young men rose from their seats.

"Sit down!" glared Captain Judkins. "I'll have no lawlessness on my ship! I invited Mr. Douglass to speak, and he shall do so as he pleases. Leave if you so choose, but anyone who touches the man will be put in irons, do I make myself clear?"

He must have, Frederick thought gleefully, *because even the sulky hands who swabbed in steerage have been very respectful to me as of late.* The rest of the voyage was one of the most pleasant journeys Frederick had ever made.

Upon arrival, the still-incensed Southerners contacted British newspapers to castigate the impudent Negro and coarse sea captain who had so offended them.

Their angry letters to the editor only inflamed many British citizens' sense of racial justice, and publicized Frederick's arrival as an American abolitionist. Opportunities for him to speak immediately opened up that would have taken months if the Southerners had not pleaded their case before the public.

Later Frederick wrote of the sense of the everyday freedom he experienced in the British Isles: "I employ a cab—I am seated beside white people—I reach the hotel—I enter the same door—I am shown into the same parlor—I dine at the same table—and no one is offended. . . . When I go to church I am met by no upturned nose and scornful lip, to tell me, 'We don't allow niggers in here.' "[1]

Frederick met many of Britain's powerful politicians: Lord Brougham and Parliament members Richard Cobden, John Bright, and Benjamin Disraeli, who later became the prime minister.

But he was overwhelmed by the eloquence of the fiery Irish leader Daniel O'Connell, who had led the fight for Irish independence from Britain for many years, and refused to accept money for his cause from slaveholders in the American South.

Frederick toured Ireland, arranging for the British publication of the *Narrative* with Richard D. Webb, a veteran supporter of the antislavery movement with whom he frequently clashed. Frederick made many friends while in Ireland, including the Thomas Jennings family, prosperous Roman Catholics who welcomed him often to their Dublin home. Ireland's most prominent temperance leader, Father Theobald Mathew, persuaded Frederick to take the temperance vow. Frederick spoke vehemently against the evils of slavery and alcohol at St. Patrick's Temperance Hall in Cork. The lord mayor of Dublin invited him for dinner and made sure Frederick saw all the beautiful, ancient buildings in his city.

He loved the hospitality of the antislavery supporters in Ireland, but the poverty of the Irish lower class disturbed him, particularly as his ardently compassionate hosts seemed oblivious to it.

How can they be so blind to the needs of their own people? Many poor here in Ireland are as miserable as the slaves in America. Much of their suffering, he thought, was directly linked to alcohol. Frederick became more active than ever in the temperance movement.

He also visited Scotland, speaking against slavery in

countless religious meetings. Thomas Chalmers, the leader of the newly formed Free Church of Scotland, hated slavery. He was a champion of the poor, many of whom languished in sweatshop conditions in Glasgow and Edinburgh. But his fledgling denomination accepted substantial contributions from many Presbyterians in the American South, and Frederick thundered against "taking the money of slave-dealers to build churches and thus extend the gospel, but of holding fellowship with the traffickers of human flesh."[2]

"SEND BACK THE MONEY!" Frederick roared to his audiences.

"SEND BACK THE MONEY!" they echoed by the thousands.

He and others so roused the Scottish people that the motto, "Send back the money!" was repeated in newspaper headlines, displayed on banners and signs, and was even sung in a popular song. Some antislavery supporters disapproved of Frederick's open attacks on Chalmers and his church, believing that fellow Christians should reasonably settle their conflicts, even if they involved slavery.

Ultimately, the Free Church decided to keep the money. But Frederick felt that he and his fellow abolitionists had captured the hearts of the volatile, freedom-loving Scots. Regardless of their religious leaders' actions, they would not accept slavery, and British disapproval, while doing little to actually free the American slaves, let Southern slave owners know that they would not achieve the international respectability they craved.

"God bless you, Frederick Douglass."

The speaker was a bent, eighty-seven-year-old man with a shaky voice and a fragile white hand that he extended to Frederick.

Can such a giant look so weak? Frederick mused. Thomas Clarkson was one of the first Englishmen to oppose slavery. Once he had single-handedly fought a whole group of racists who had attempted to push him into the ocean. He and his colleagues had pioneered a movement that had shaken the British colonial empire. Because of their efforts, most of the world was rid of the curse of slavery. Now Frederick, William Lloyd Garrison, and George Thompson, a prominent young British abolitionist, listened to his benediction.

"God bless you, Frederick Douglass!" Clarkson repeated. "I have given sixty years of my life to the emancipation of your people, and if I had sixty years more they should all be given to the same cause.[3] You must continue the fight, Mr. Douglass, until every slave on this sad planet is free."

Frederick and the other young men stood spellbound.

I have met British lords and ladies, noble Christian clerics, generous philanthropists, and brilliant scholars dedicated to the cause of freedom, thought Frederick, *but not one of them is as great as Thomas Clarkson.*

"Frederick, the Society and I believe that you should remain in England a while longer." William Lloyd Garrison smiled apologetically. "I know it has been over a year since you last saw your family, and we regret to make such a request. But your work here has reaped rich rewards. All Britain is willing to listen to our cause!"

"I love England," answered Frederick. "To remain here would not difficult. But I wrote Anna and the children just the other day that we would soon be together."

Frederick considered sending for his family and living permanently in England. But would the aristocratic English intellectuals who had so gladly received him also welcome

145

his dark-skinned, uneducated wife? His black children? Frederick wanted to believe that they would. But were the enormous adjustments of living in a foreign land worth the risk? Who would help Anna make all the necessary arrangements? Frederick's sister Harriet had remained with his family and corresponded regularly with him, as Anna could not. But now Harriet had informed him that she was soon to be married and must lead her own life.

"I must go home," said Frederick.

"We are also more concerned than ever about your safety," said Garrison. "Your *Narrative* continues to sell briskly, and you are now as well-known in the States as you are in Great Britain. I do not think your former masters could enslave you without enormous difficulty; but such action is still legal. Your speeches that describe their evil treatment have doubtless inflamed them.

"Buffum has agreed to return to the States to care for your family in your extended absence," Garrison went on. "We would hope to send you back next spring, when some of the furor from the *Narrative* has subsided."

Frederick finally returned to the United States in April 1847; but he did so as a free man, unafraid, for the first time in his life, of recapture.

"Mr. Douglass," said Ellen Richardson, "I find it unthinkable that you should return to your native land in fear of your very life." Ellen, a Quaker, and the headmistress of a school for girls, was an outspoken opponent of slavery. "My sister-in-law Anna and I would beg you to accept the gifts of your devoted British friends who feel as we do—that you must return to your country emancipated and fully able to do the noble work to which you have been called." She handed a stunned Frederick an envelope full of bank notes. "My brother, Mr. Henry Richardson, is a lawyer, and believes arrangements can be made to produce such a result."

Nothing could stop Ellen, marveled Frederick as he sailed home. *Nothing. My friend White—such a friend! I will never forget his willingness to defend me from that Indiana mob—contacted Ellis Gray Loring, who had excellent influence in high places. The Honorable Walter Forward of Pennsylvania also used his power on my behalf. They contracted with Walter Lowrie of New York, who knew exactly which lawyer to hire in Baltimore. Captain Auld had sold his rights to me to Hugh, who asked a high price for my freedom: a hundred fifty pounds sterling, or one thousand, two hundred fifty dollars! But my dear friends paid him without one moment's hesitation.*

Not everyone celebrated Frederick's new freedom. "Some of my uncompromising anti-slavery friends. . .failed to see the wisdom of this commercial transaction, and were not pleased that I consented to it, even by my silence," Frederick wrote later. "They thought it a violation of anti-slavery principles, conceding the right of property in man, and a wasteful expenditure of money. For myself, viewing it simply in the light of a ransom, or as money extorted by a robber, and my liberty of more value than one hundred and fifty pounds sterling, I could not see either a violation of the laws of morality or of economy."[4]

I was sorry to lose Henry Wright's friendship, thought Frederick regretfully. *Mary Welsh—how I will miss our discussions in her lovely home in Edinburgh. I am sorry we parted as opponents when we have worked so closely together for the cause.*

But they cannot possibly know what it is like to scan an audience for those with Covey's eyes, wondering if another "nigger-breaker" is in our midst. They cannot understand what it is like to awaken in the night, feeling the lash. They do not walk on Sunday afternoons, still alert, after these eight years of freedom, to furtive movements in shadowed doorways and alleys. . . .

Unthinkable that a mere fragment of paper could make such a momentous difference in a man's life.

Frederick knew the sale documents were carefully deposited in the ship's safe. He wished he could hold the precious bill of sale in his hand to reassure himself that he was indeed free. But Frederick had already read it so many times that he had almost memorized it:

To all whom it may concern: Be it known that I, Hugh Auld of the city of Baltimore, in Baltimore County in the State of Maryland, for divers good causes and considerations me thereunto moving, have released from slavery, liberated, manumitted, and set free, and by these presents do hereby release from slavery, liberate, manumit, and set free, MY NEGRO MAN named FREDERICK BAI-LEY, otherwise called DOUGLASS, being of the age of twenty-eight years or thereabouts, and able to work and gain a sufficient livelihood and main-tenance; and him, the said negro man named FREDERICK DOUGLASS, I do declare to be henceforth free, manumitted, and discharged from all manner of servitude to me, my executors and administrators forever.[5]

Forever. I am free forever. Thanks be to God!

thirteen

I have decided to go through with it," said Frederick.

His words were met with dead silence. Edmund Quincy, the brusque editor of the *National Anti-Slavery Standard,* the official publication of the American Anti-Slavery Association, scowled; Maria Weston Chapman, the powerful secretary of the organization, glanced sharply at William Lloyd Garrison, who set his elegant teacup down on Mrs. Chapman's mahogany table.

"Frederick, we respect your desire to start your own newspaper," he said sincerely. "We have the highest opinion of your talents. But we think they would best serve the cause if you would continue to lecture; your power of oratory, my friend, is unmatched."

Frederick knew Garrison was not trying to manipulate him; he had helped Frederick grow from a stammering amateur to an articulate spokesman for freedom. It had been hard for Garrison to see Frederick's fame supersede his own, but unlike other members of the Society, both black and white, the man had not become entangled in jealousy.

"Yes, Mr. Douglass," said Mrs. Chapman, "certainly you would wish to give your best for the cause of liberty for your people. A newspaper is a difficult enterprise—"

"It is," growled Quincy. Tea parties were not to his liking, and Frederick's stubbornness interfered with his desire for a good cigar. "It involves editorial, business, and printing skills—not to mention financial backing!"

"I have sufficient means to start the paper," said Frederick quietly.

Maria frowned; she had received numerous letters from Frederick's English friends, mostly women. Many of them appeared to be quite wealthy, even titled. The independence he was displaying must have its roots in them.

"But you have never edited a paper," soothed Garrison. "I can tell you that it will challenge you more than anything you have ever conceived."

Frederick paused. Garrison, again, was not speaking idly; he had edited *The Liberator* for many years, and the prominent abolitionist paper had never been completely self-supporting. Maria Chapman and her antislavery bazaars came to Garrison's rescue annually. How could an upstart paper, edited by a black man who had never spent a day in a schoolhouse, succeed?

"We could use some articles from you in the *Standard,*" said Quincy grudgingly.

"And more in the *Liberator,*" added Garrison. "We have not heard enough from you yet, Frederick." He smiled. "And supporters all over the United States beg for your presence in their churches and lecture halls. Please reconsider."

Abashed by Garrison's opposition, Frederick finally

nodded. Other colleagues, including Wendell Phillips, applauded his decision.

But he did not forget about it.

Frederick dashed from the train station at Lynn, Massachusetts, ignoring, for once, a crowd of devotees who greeted him there.

"Pa! Pa!" Seven-year-old Lewis Henry ran madly towards Frederick, who kneeled and threw his arms around his son. Five-year-old Frederick followed slowly, his sparkling eyes intent on his father's face.

I have been in Britain for almost two years. No wonder he is hesitant. Does he remember me at all?

Frederick opened his arms, and the little boy snuggled contentedly under his chin. Frederick carried him home, with Lewis in hand, hopping like an ecstatic little frog.

Will she welcome me?

"My dear Anna," said Frederick. She stood in the door of their house, wearing her usual cotton gown and bright bandanna, her dark eyes searching his. Then, slowly, she held her hands out to her husband, who held her close.

"I was afraid to think it true," she whispered.

"I will call it the *North Star,*" said Frederick. "The North Star points the way to many a traveler on the underground railroad. I hope that my newspaper will provide the same sure guidance for all who read it."

Encouraged by his English friends and Gerrit Smith, a white abolitionist who became a major contributor, he decided to take a momentous step. Frederick visited Rochester, New York, where he had lectured before, and bought a printing press and other equipment with the four thousand dollars that British friends had raised. Perhaps if he moved well away from the Boston area, his paper would not compete for subscriptions and undermine Garrison's *Liberator.*

His action angered many of his American Anti-Slavery colleagues. Garrison was hurt at Frederick's failure to heed his advice. Frederick was sorry to lose his position as lecturer for the Society. He appreciated all they had done for him, and considered most of the members his dear friends.

But the Society was far from perfect. Despite its noble motto of social equality, the Society had its own brand of racism. Money matters were often delegated to whites only, and the real power rested in their hands. Frederick felt as if the Society had done little for his family while he was touring as a lecturer. His book eventually earned profits that assured their well-being. But if Anna had not taken in sewing before its success, his children would have suffered.

Too, some of Frederick's fellow lecturers were uncomfortable with sharing accommodations with him; others were paternalistic and condescending, he felt. Some even urged him to adopt a less educated speaking style so that his hearers would believe he was once actually a slave.

"Give us the facts," John Collins, the head of the Society, had once said, "and we will take care of the philosophy."[1]

But Frederick had studied, read, pondered, and matured. His personal convictions burned inside him.

A newspaper, expressing an independent black point of view, was essential.

"Move?" Anna stopped kneading her bread and stared at Frederick. "Move again?"

Frederick quailed a little at the anger in her eyes. "Rochester is a lovely, progressive town; there are many black families there. It will be a good place for our children to grow up."

"Lynn, Massachusetts, is a good place for them to grow up." She spoke slowly; her words were the red-hot flow from a volcano. "You have not been here much, but it is the only home they remember."

Anna turned away and pounded the dough silently.

For once, Frederick could not think of anything to say.

There is much more to starting a newspaper than I thought. Garrison was certainly correct.

Frederick moved to Rochester alone, promising to return for his family as soon as the business was established. The new venture excited him.

John Dick, a Britisher who soon arrived to assist him, decided Frederick's costly printing press did not fit their needs; they had to hire William Clough to print the paper.

Rent, postage, various sundry expenses—it is all far more costly than I had estimated. Thank heaven our good abolitionist friends give us free room and board. I dare not take out more than a dollar or two at a time as a salary.

Although Frederick had not found a home for them yet, the rest of the family followed in the winter of 1848, boarding with various antislavery sympathizers. The arrangements infuriated Anna more than ever. She missed her own kitchen and parlor in Lynn; she craved privacy. Constant visiting, even with Frederick's courteous, respectful friends, was a trial for her.

But the situation improved by spring. Frederick bought a pleasant house with nine rooms and a large front porch from an abolitionist family in Rochester who ignored the commotion the transaction created in the all-white neighborhood. Anna was relieved; finally, enough room for her lively family! And she was ecstatic as she dug into the soil in the backyard and critically studied the patterns of

153

sunshine there: this was a prime garden spot!

Gerrit Smith's wife, another dedicated gardener, tried to befriend Anna with gifts of seeds and bulbs and conversations about planting times and harvesting seasons. Amy Post, the wife of Isaiah, both lifelong, close friends of Frederick's in Rochester, asked her for one of her prize pumpkins to serve as Cinderella's coach in a school play.

Anna said no. These were Frederick's white friends. Rochester was his world, not hers. When his educated, often famous guests arrived for dinner, she cooked them elegant meals, but never ate with them and her husband. She chose to remain in the kitchen.

But she could not resist being drawn into a secret world, an underground network in Rochester known only to a few.

When she heard one loud and one soft knock at her back door, Anna was there immediately to open it. Her soup pot constantly simmered; she always had a clean blanket to offer the desperate runaway slaves whose haunted eyes soon filled with tears of gratitude at the quiet woman's help. Sometimes only two or three, sometimes a dozen—Anna fed and quickly sheltered them all in her cellar, attic, or barn loft, where they rested for a few hours before moving on to the next underground railroad station and, hopefully, freedom in Canada.

Remembering her help in obtaining his own freedom, Frederick loved her for it. His own involvement gave him a sense of satisfaction unequalled by anything else. "True, as a means of destroying slavery, it was like an attempt to bail out the ocean with a teaspoon, but the thought that there was one less slave, and one more freeman—having myself been a slave, and a fugitive slave—brought to my heart unspeakable joy."[2]

The underground railroad was usually more exhausting

than exciting; most activity took place at night, and Frederick and Anna often faced busy days at office and home with groggy, aching heads. But at times, the danger of their nocturnal pastime was all too apparent.

"I must see Mr. Douglass!"

Frederick was surprised to see the dignified, bespectacled face of Bradford Wellington burst through his office door.

"Sir," said the lawyer in a barely discernible whisper, "a slave hunter is in the office of the United States commissioner this instant. He seeks documents that will enable him to recapture the three young men you have hidden, and he will obtain them immediately, I am sure!"

"Thank you, sir!" Frederick had no idea how the prominent man had known about the runaways, or why he had chosen to help them, but Wellington's face had the open look Frederick had come to trust. In any case, he had no choice but to believe the lawyer was telling the truth. "Good day, and may God bless you."

"Simon," Frederick called the elderly black man who did odd jobs around his office. "Please take this message to Mrs. Douglass immediately. Then ride to Asa Anthony's farm. There is so little time! Whom else can I send?"

"My boy Charlie can go wherever you want," said Simon.

"Thank heaven! Please ask him to ride his fastest horse to Farmington to this house," Frederick gave directions, "and, of course, no one is to speak a word about this!"

"Yessir," answered Simon. He exited much faster than his age would warrant.

Frederick headed for J. P. Morris's office; the Rochester businessman quietly collected funds from black and white, Democrat and Whig alike, to help finance the runaways' trips across Lake Ontario to St. Catharines, Canada.

Frederick also raised funds, particularly among his generous English friends. But he had to avoid public contact with runaways; he was notorious already for his antislavery activities, and the fines and prison terms for helping escapees were very real. So J. P. drove to the landing, purchased three tickets, and walked casually along the shore. An hour later a wagon appeared in the distance. Three young black men, dressed like servants, hoisted large trunks to their shoulders and boarded the steamship. J. P. gave them instructions regarding the baggage and a nonexistent relative in St. Catharines, and the three nodded obediently. He resisted the temptation to wave as the boat cut through the chilly waters. They stared at their feet, eyes blank and proper.

Not too long, now, boys, thought J.P. *You will soon breathe the sweet, free air of Canada.*

"What do you mean, child?" Frederick bent incredulously toward his daughter. "You say you are not allowed to learn with the other girls?"

"I am not allowed in the same room with them, Papa," answered Rosetta, her eyes filling with tears. "Oh, I am doing well in school," she reassured him with a shaky smile that broke his heart. "But I may not learn in the same room with the other girls, and I must take my recess when they are inside, because I am colored."

Frederick dried her tears, promising to remedy the situation at Miss Tracy's School for Young Ladies. Fortunately, her brothers came rioting in, and Rosetta, with practiced ease, set about putting them in their place. Frederick, with a wave good-bye, set about doing the same with Miss Tracy.

"Have you indeed isolated my daughter from her schoolmates, Miss Tracy? When I enrolled her in your school, I understood no such condition." If Miss Tracy had been familiar with Frederick's oratorical style, she would have known that his subdued voice was only a prelude to the thunderous tones that made his opponents cringe.

"Indeed, sir, I had to, as the trustees objected to her admission. They have done so much for my school. I thought that if we adopted this arrangement for a term, my pupils would adjust to her—"

"Then the other girls have objected to her presence."

"Well, no."

"Perhaps, then, you should ask them." Frederick drew himself up to his full height and glared down at the startled woman. "I have no doubt that such blatant prejudice does not flourish in their young hearts as it does in your own. I will *not* allow my daughter to be so treated; the WORLD SHALL HEAR OF YOUR DISGRACEFUL BEHAVIOR, MADAM!" Frederick jammed his hat on and stormed out of the school, leaving the schoolmistress openmouthed.

Surely he is wrong. I am a Christian, in good standing with my church. My family and I are known for our charitable deeds.

But Frederick's angry words lingered. The next morning, she questioned her other pupils: "If Rosetta came back to our class, where would she sit?"

"She could sit by me!" "No, me!" "I want to sit by Rosetta!"

Flustered at their replies, the headmistress wrote each parent to ask if he objected to Rosetta's presence.

Only one did—H. G. Warner, the editor of the *Rochester Courier.* And Rosetta was asked to leave.

Frederick enrolled his daughter elsewhere, but he had only begun to fight. Black children in Rochester were automatically sent to the inferior colored schools. Frederick refused to do so, engaging a tutor. He then haunted every

157

Board of Education meeting, objecting as a citizen and a taxpayer to such segregation. Men like Isaac Post, Benjamin Fish, and Asa Anthony rose to support him.

Not everyone in Rochester rejoiced in Frederick's campaign for racial equality. Some regarded the *North Star* as an embarrassment, and the New York *Herald* suggested that area citizens should toss Frederick's printing press into Lake Ontario and chase him off to Canada. But while many Rochester citizens did not support him, many came to understand him during the twenty-five years he spent in their town. The city, which had imposed racial barriers to education, cultural activities, and entertainments, eventually lifted the restrictions.

Frederick remained in contact with his old friends from the Anti-Slavery Society and continued to support their point of view in the *North Star,* but he rarely lectured for them. He desperately needed funds to support his family and keep the paper afloat. He wrote and edited all day, then took trains to surrounding cities such as Victor, Farmington, and Buffalo to speak. Late at night he once more boarded the train and rode home, only to face a similar day within a few hours. Stress took its toll on the novice editor and his family; Frederick's new baby girl, Annie, did not recognize him when he tried to hold her. It also took its toll on the *North Star* itself. Frederick publicized his paper everywhere he traveled, but subscription increase alone did not solve its many business problems. In fact, the newspaper's growth only caused things to pile up more. He was deeply in debt, having mortgaged his house to pay the *North Star's* regular operating costs.

Were they right when they said the North Star *was doomed to failure?*

They were not, asserted Julia Griffiths. Julia, an eccentric, outspoken abolitionist, was a friend of Ellen and Anna Richardson, the Englishwomen who had spearheaded the effort to purchase Frederick's freedom. Frederick had met her shortly before he left England; they had written regularly ever since. When problems threatened to destroy the *North Star*, Julia arrived with her sister Eliza to help; she brought business savvy and innovation to the scene. Under her supervision, the *North Star* achieved four thousand subscriptions from all over the world. Frederick continued his long work days, but had more time to enjoy new friends.

Among these was Susan B. Anthony, a feminist neighbor who regularly filled her parlor with controversial people. Frederick enjoyed the stimulation of evenings at the Anthony household. He met and corresponded with some of the most prominent women of his time, including another feminist leader, Elizabeth Cady Stanton, abolitionist Lucretia Coffin Mott, and Harriet Beecher Stowe, who first wrote him while researching her book *Uncle Tom's Cabin*.

But it was his friendship with Gerrit Smith that would ultimately affect him the most. Smith was a wealthy white abolitionist from Peterboro, New York, who owned large tracts of property which he gave away to landless blacks, whom he regarded as the most disadvantaged class of people in the U.S. Smith belonged to the Liberty Party, a new radical group that espoused, above all, freedom for slaves. Frederick had a high opinion of Smith, but disagreed with him in his approach to abolishing slavery. Frederick had been schooled in the Garrisonian viewpoint: Political action would never free the slaves; abolitionists should depend on moral and spiritual power only to accomplish that end. Smith felt that all concerned people should join the Liberty Party and elect a president who would free the slaves. But the men had

159

a great deal of respect for each other. Smith became one of the *North Star's* main contributors, and the two wrote each other often, to the consternation of Frederick's American Anti-Slavery Society associates. Smith introduced Frederick to his many political friends, and Frederick found himself speaking at their meetings and listening to their arguments.

Finally, what Garrison feared most came to pass: Frederick reconsidered and changed his position to match that of Gerrit Smith.

He declared his decision in a speech at the annual meeting of the American Anti-Slavery Society. William Lloyd Garrison stared in stunned disbelief; Wendell Phillips, William Quincy, and the others were filled with rage. Frederick left the platform, hearing his own footsteps echo in the stony silence.

Frederick merged the *North Star* with Smith's paper, the *Liberty Party Paper,* and re-named it *Frederick Douglass's Paper.*

Frederick, who had watched the political arena from afar, began to publish news articles that urged action by the president, Congress, and voters to end slavery.

The Liberator, meanwhile, published public condemnations of Frederick's new paper and policies. Frederick blasted Garrison in his newspaper for his refusal to strengthen the antislavery movement by joining with other abolitionist groups that did not follow Garrisonian practices. Both demeaned each other to all their mutual acquaintances, who attempted to pacify the once best friends. But attempts at reconciliation exploded into even greater hostilities. In a November 1853 issue, Garrison's *Liberator* stated that Julia Griffiths, Frederick's business manager, was a threat to the Douglass marriage.

All of Frederick's friends had initially been grateful for

Griffiths's managerial expertise. They knew that Frederick spent most of his time on idealistic and literary concerns; he was often neglectful of practical ones. Many of them were also women's rights advocates, so they saw no difficulty in Julia's capable supervision of the paper. But even for the white abolitionists, the sight of a black man and a white woman together, even in a workplace, was difficult to accept. The fact that Julia and her sister Eliza lived with the Douglasses for a while also raised eyebrows. But when Eliza, who traveled with Frederick and Julia on many business and lecture trips, married and moved away, abolitionist leaders knew that Frederick's credibility and their cause would suffer if they worked, lived in the same house and occasionally traveled together as before—which they did, apparently unperturbed by their aghast colleagues. When old friends approached Frederick about the impropriety of such a relationship, he dismissed the criticism as unimportant. He, alone, as a free man, was morally responsible for his choices. Julia had moved to her own house two months before all the commotion broke loose, he said, and anyone who wished to observe the two could do so during business hours. Julia was a family friend, as well as a personal one. She often had tea in the kitchen with Anna, who rarely associated with her husband's colleagues. Julia had even attempted to teach Anna to read, but was as unsuccessful as the many tutors he had hired.

Now, enraged by Garrison's accusations, Frederick published a letter dictated by Anna, denying them. In later articles he declared that Garrison had no business dragging his family into their quarrel and charged him with racism. Garrison, in turn, attacked Frederick in *The Liberator* as an ungrateful heretic and betrayer.

Harriet Beecher Stowe finally managed to calm the

storm. She questioned Frederick as to his new views and found he could defend them well; it was not because of some motive of ingratitude or vindictiveness that he had changed camps, she told Garrison. And when the times were so critical for the antislavery cause, why was Garrison publishing unproven hearsay? Her common sense approach cooled both combatants to a semi-civil level; they published no more blatantly inflammatory articles about each other. Julia Griffiths continued to work for Frederick Douglass, but returned to England less than two years later and married a minister.

fourteen

This Fourth of July is *yours*, not *mine*. *You* may rejoice, *I* must mourn. To drag a man in fetters into the grand illuminated temple of liberty, and call upon him to join you in joyous anthems, were inhuman mockery and sacrilegious irony. Do you mean, citizens, to mock me, by asking me to speak today?"[1]

The well-dressed, complacent holiday crowd, fresh from picnics and parades, could not have been more startled if Frederick had shot a cannon into their midst. Ladies in pastel lawn dresses stared at Frederick, their frightened eyes peering from beneath summer bonnets. Men sat bolt upright, tight Sunday best forgotten in their surprise and anger.

"If so, there is a parallel to your conduct. And let me warn you that it is dangerous to copy the example of a nation whose crimes, towering up to heaven, were thrown down by the breath of the Almighty, burying that nation in irrecoverable ruin! I can today take up the plaintive lament of a peeled and woe-smitten people."

Frederick went on, echoing the pain of another people,

the Israelites, who suffered the despair of slavery.

"By the rivers of Babylon, there we sat down. Yea! we wept when we remembered Zion. We hanged our harps upon the willows in the midst thereof. For there, they that carried us away captive, required of us a song; and they who wasted us required of us mirth, saying, 'Sing us one of the songs of Zion.' How can we sing the Lord's song in a strange land? If I forget thee, O Jerusalem, let my right hand forget her cunning. If I do not remember thee, let my tongue cleave to the roof of my mouth.

"Fellow-citizens, above your national, tumultuous joy, I hear the mournful wail of millions, whose chains, heavy and grievous yesterday, are today rendered more intolerable by the jubilant shouts that reach them. If I do forget, if I do not faithfully remember those bleeding children of sorrow this day, 'may my right hand forget her cunning, and may my tongue cleave to the roof of my mouth!' To forget them, to pass lightly over their wrongs, and to chime in with the popular theme, would be treason most scandalous and shocking, and would make a me a reproach before God and the world. . . .

"Standing with God and the crushed and bleeding slave on this occasion, I will, in the name of humanity which is outraged, in the name of liberty which is fettered, in the name of the Constitution and the Bible, which are disregarded and trampled upon, dare to call in question and to denounce, with all the emphasis I can command, everything that serves to perpetuate slavery—the great sin and shame of America! . . .[2]

"What to the American slave is your Fourth of July? I answer, a day that reveals to him, more than all other days in the year, the gross injustice and cruelty to which he is the constant victim. . . . There is not a nation on the earth guilty of practices more shocking and bloody, than are the people of these United States, at this very hour."[3]

A summer evening breeze blew through the Corinthian Hall in Rochester; in the deep quiet following Frederick's speech every person in the packed-in crowd could hear its whispers. The Ladies' Anti-Slavery Society members, who had asked him to speak, dared not look at each other. Would the people of Rochester demand that the Corinthian Hall be closed after such a tirade? But Frederick's friends and neighbors rose as one, clapping, applauding what they knew was an indictment against their own apathy, as well as a damning accusation against slave owners.

Their Fourth of July celebrations would never be the same.

"Frederick, is God dead?"[4]

Frederick faced the piercing eyes of his old friend, Sojourner Truth. She was a fearless, vocal advocate of freedom for her people, and a Christian of deep integrity. Like William Lloyd Garrison, she was against the use of political action for her cause. Sojourner was appalled, as Frederick had expected, at the speech he had just made. Frederick had told the crowd in Salem, Ohio, that he feared that slaves would not be freed without bloodshed.

"Frederick, is God dead?" she repeated fiercely, her grandmotherly face shining with anger.

"No, my dear sister," Frederick answered gently, "and because God is not dead, slavery can only end in blood."[5]

As Frederick had become more and more involved in politics, he sensed the growing tensions in the country. He had attended the Free Soil Party Convention in 1848, marveling at the wholehearted commitment of his white brothers to the freedom of the black slaves. He rejoiced in the superb oratory of fellow blacks: Henry Highland Garnet, Charles L. Remond, Henry Bibb, and Samuel Ringold Ward, the best speaker of them all, Frederick thought, himself included.

"Antislavery thus far had only been sheet-lightning; the Buffalo convention sought to make it a thunderbolt," wrote Frederick.[6] The tiny Liberty party did not have the power to make the Southern slaveholders take notice; the Free Soil party did. Although its presidential candidate, Martin van Buren (who had already served a term as president) did not win, the South was shaken. Some even demanded a president from the North and one from the South, with legislation passing only when the two were unanimous in their vetoes and signatures on new laws. Congressional sessions resembled a savage tug-of-war.

Eventually the Southern states won the passage of the Fugitive Slave Law of 1850, which demanded that all U.S. citizens had to return any runaway slave to his rightful owner on the word of only two witnesses.

Many of Frederick's distinguished colleagues who were former slaves left for Canada. Others agonized over the decision to run or stay. Frederick knew his position was far less desperate, as he held legal freedman's papers; but he felt no black person was safe while such a law was in force. The loss of his coworkers devastated him. Would the slaveholders try to "prove" he was not a freedman? Would they attempt to steal his family? Would slavery prevail forever, after all?

Shortly before the Free Soil Party had held its momentous convention, Captain John Brown, a former military man turned storekeeper, had invited Frederick to his home. Rev. Henry Garnet had spoken highly of him, so Frederick went to Springfield, Massachusetts, to meet him. Impressed by the grandness of his store, Frederick expected to visit an equally elegant mansion; he was disappointed to find the Brown family living in a very modest home with minimal furnishings and no servants. But Captain Brown, a wiry New Englander with blue-gray eyes that glittered with the strength of his convictions, had reasons for his restrained lifestyle. He wanted to create a small armed group of dedicated men who would live in the Appalachian Mountains, induce slaves to follow them to freedom there, then train and arm them for resistance. Such an endeavor, Brown knew, would be quite expensive. Therefore, he and his deeply religious family had sacrificed for years, preparing for the time when the plan would become reality.

A stunned Frederick asked Brown question after question.

"Can we not appeal to the slave owners' hearts? Can we not convert them to the truth of the Bible, sir, that God made all men and would see them all free?"

John Brown looked incredulously at Frederick. "We would convert them if we could, you and I," he said softly. "But," the light glittered in his eyes again, "I know their arrogant hearts; no one will persuade them to free their slaves. No, Mr. Douglass," he shook his head emphatically, "slavery will never end without war."

"Even if the worst came," Brown said, "I could but be killed, and I have no better use for my life than to lay it down in the cause of the slave."[7]

Brown's words had haunted Frederick ever since. Day and night he pondered his country's struggles.

The South breathes threats toward those who rescue their slaves.

The North shakes its fist at those who dare to force slavery on our country.

The new territories are full of violence as slave owners and abolitionists settle on neighboring farms.

How can God's justice prevail? Slavery can only end with the shedding of blood.

Frederick's days were never long enough. He lectured against slavery nationwide, as well as promoting the temperance movement and women's rights. He continued to shelter runaways, including three slaves who had killed their former master when he attempted to recapture them. Frederick campaigned for presidential candidates Gerrit Smith and later, John C. Fremont. He raised money for John Brown's new plan to lead a small military force to Kansas to keep slaveholders out of that territory. Frederick labored diligently on *My Bondage and My Freedom,* a more complete autobiography which quickly sold fifteen thousand copies in two months. He also worked extensively with Ottilia Assing, a European journalist who eventually translated his latest autobiography into German.

"You are going again?"

Frederick nodded. His mind was busy cataloging dates, lecture invitations, train tickets, notes—he hardly noticed Anna's presence.

"The children are growing," said Anna. "Rosetta, Lewis, Frederick—they are all in their teens. Charles and Annie are no longer small. One day you will come home, and they will not be here."

Frederick stared. It was Anna's longest speech in months.

"If I do not fight, they will live in a world that permits slavery. I *can't* let that happen, Anna."

She sighed. "Where is your tour this time?"

"New York. I'll be in New Jersey, too."

Anna stiffened. "I suppose you will see Ottilia?"

Frederick frowned. "Anna, it is important that *My Bondage and My Freedom* be translated for our European benefactors. Without their interest, their generosity, our cause would indeed suffer."

Anna was silent.

"If you so dislike my meeting with Ottilia in Hoboken, perhaps she can come here more often. She would like to know you better."

"Of course."

Frederick looked at his wife sharply, but her eyes told him nothing.

Anna went downstairs and out to her garden. She began to weed.

Stacks of mail! Frederick sighed. *But that is good; it means people are reading our paper.* He spotted an envelope with John Brown's handwriting on it. *Better open this now, before the others arrive this morning; ever since Kansas, John is in hiding.*

John Brown and his sons had moved to Kansas when that territory was opened to slavery. Brown and Frederick both saw the escalating tension there as an unofficial guerilla war, and Brown as an agent of justice, a fighter for righteousness. Four hundred Missouri troops vowed to never return home until they had forced all abolitionists out of Kansas; Brown and his thirty men made them reconsider. He also raided several slaveholding farms in Missouri and helped twelve runaways escape to Canada, despite a nation-wide manhunt. The federal government filed charges against Brown and searched for him and his men in vain.

"My dear Douglass, I am convinced that now is the time to strike," the letter read. Brown went on to ask Frederick to meet him at an old stone quarry in Chambersburg,

Pennsylvania, with any funds he could raise quickly.

Frederick immediately took a train to Chambersburg. He was recognized almost immediately by a local official and requested to speak in the town hall. To avoid suspicion, Frederick agreed. Brown's secretary, Mr. Kagi, contacted him, and the next morning a barber, Henry Watson, directed them to an overgrown road that led to the stone quarry. Frederick and Kagi approached the meeting place carefully; they had no doubt that Brown was well-armed and monitoring every sound in the countryside. A fisherman sat by the edge of the water, indolently checking his line, his weather-beaten hat drooping around his shaggy gray head. It was John Brown—a worn, apprehensive-looking Brown.

His eyes have the hunted look of an animal, thought Frederick. *But I do not see one waver of compromise in them.*

Indeed, Brown had decided to attack Harper's Ferry, a federal arsenal in Virginia. He invited Frederick to join him.

"A federal arsenal! My dear colleague, do you know what you are saying? Such an act would be suicidal!" Frederick stared at Brown in disbelief.

A faint twinkle appeared in the weary gray-blue eyes. "The federal government is already hot on my trail, but has not captured me yet."

"Nevertheless, such a plan is madness! You would inflame the entire country against the abolitionist cause!"

"It appears to me," said Brown mildly, "that rousing is just what this country needs. If my brave men and I capture Harper's Ferry (we have beaten a few odds before, you know) and hold prominent citizens hostage, we have a fighting chance of holding the arsenal." His eyes glittered with the old fanatical light. "The slaves will rally to our cause. Uprisings will explode everywhere in the South, and the day of your people's jubilee will be at hand."

"You are serious," said Frederick in disbelief. "The imaginary military defenses you drew on pine boards for my children's play—"

"They never were imaginary," said John Brown.

"You must listen to me, my friend," said Frederick. Frederick begged Brown to return to his old plan of placing a militia in the Appalachian Mountains to assist escaping slaves. It was a far more feasible scheme, Frederick argued, and would help accomplish their goal without openly attacking the federal government. Brown listened willingly, but refused to change his mind, even though Frederick pleaded with him.

Frederick finally rose to leave. John Brown threw his arms around his friend.

"Come with me, Douglass; I will defend you with my life. I want you for a special purpose. When I strike, the bees will begin to swarm, and I shall want you to help hive them."[8]

Frederick was so choked with emotion he could only shake his head.

Do I refuse because attacking Harper's Ferry is the wrong thing to do? Or am I a coward? Is the old soldier a madman, or he is the only sane one in our midst? O God in heaven, I cannot believe this is the thing to do. . . .

"Good-bye, John Brown. May God have mercy upon you." Frederick turned to go, tears blurring the green forest path before him.

"Mr. Douglass! Mr. Douglass!" Heavy fists pounded on the door of his room.

Frederick looked up wearily from his novel. He had spoken several times to large crowds in the great National

171

Hall in Philadelphia. His usual fatigue had been exacerbated by the news that John Brown had indeed attacked Harper's Ferry and was fighting federal troops led by Colonel Robert E. Lee. Anxiety had drained every last ounce of strength from Frederick. Was someone bringing him the news of his friend's death?

John Hern, a young telegraph operator, gasped, "Mr. Douglass! You must leave immediately!"

"Whatever is the matter?"

"Sir, Lee has captured John Brown. Among his effects they found letters to yourself, as well as to Mr. Gerrit Smith, and others. Sir, they think you were involved in this raid! I received word only minutes ago that warrants for your arrests have gone out. You must leave now!"

The turbulent gray ocean stretched in every direction. Icy November rain pelted Frederick, but he could not bring himself to go below to his dry, but claustrophobic, cabin. He needed to liberate his lungs and spirit from the tightness that had paralyzed them now for weeks.

How he had enjoyed his first voyage to England, fourteen years before! Despite his friends' concern after his first book was published, he had sensed no immediate danger.

But, now. . . Frederick's stomach churned as violently as the waves. *I thought they would arrest me as I tried to take the Walnut Street ferry in Philadelphia to Camden. No one would accompany me, save good old Franklin Turner. Even when the ferry was delayed, and we thought the U.S. marshals would soon have us both in irons, he stayed with me. Such a friend, O Lord. I thought I would never make it to New York City. Then—that horrible night at Mrs. Marks's boardinghouse in Hoboken. I could not even pretend to sleep. The papers the next day were full of it, all of the efforts to arrest those "involved" and charge them with treason. Brown had left his papers with me for safekeeping. Thank God, B. F. Blackall got the message to Lewis to destroy all of them.* Frederick managed a sickly grin. He had not consciously cultivated telegraph operators as friends, but it certainly paid to do so. *Ottilia and Johnson sneaked me to the train station, and I finally made it home. But such news! Lieutenant Governor Selden informed me that the New York governor intended to send me to Virginia to face charges! I would not have hesitated to face a jury from New York. But Virginia, where brave, foolish Brown languishes in prison, critically wounded, charged with treason! They will not rest until he is hanged.* Frederick stared at the endless pounding of the waves on the *Scotia's* deck.

So I hugged Anna, and I held my children close to my heart. I cannot forget their young faces, watching their father run like a criminal, perhaps for his life. . . .

O Mighty God who knows all, will I ever see them again?

fifteen

U pon his arrival, Frederick found all England talking about the raid on Harper's Ferry. When John Brown was executed on December 2, 1859, after a quick trial, outrage rocked the country, and lecture invitations poured in. Frederick grieved deeply for his friend, but took comfort in making impassioned speeches in antislavery meetings all over Great Britain.

During those busy months, he took time to see old friends, among them, Julia Griffiths Crofts and her husband, the Reverend H. O. Crofts, in Yorkshire. Frederick was in the midst of preparations for his journey to France when a letter from his sister Harriet arrived.

Annie, Frederick's youngest child, had died after an illness.

Annie. My little Annie. Gone. Frederick could see the dancing brown eyes, the curly black braids with red ribbons, the smile that warmed his home on the most bleak day.

One day you will come home, and they will not be here.

174

A church bell sounded outside Frederick's window, then another. Deep, slow, deliberate notes that struck his quivering heart again and again.

They will not be here.

They will not be here.

One day you will come home, and they will not be here.

Frederick sailed to Portland, Maine, on the first steamship available, and returned to Rochester through Canada. He did not leave his home for over a month.

Ralph Waldo Emerson had prophesied that John Brown's hanging would turn him into a martyr; Frederick found he was right. Northerners sang "John Brown's Body," remembering his fearless demeanor in the face of death. He insisted that his action had been solely his responsibility. No one, said Brown, had initiated the raid with him. A congressional committee, largely composed of Southerners, examined witness after witness, but discovered no substantial evidence of a widespread plot of insurrection. Embarrassed, the committee disbanded, and the North resounded with incensed triumph. Frederick cautiously came out of his self-imposed hiding, judging the worst danger was over.

Action was an excellent antidote for grief, and action was needed. His own newspaper had suffered greatly in his absence. He decided to publish only a monthly edition instead of a weekly. The presidential campaign of 1860 was heating up, and Frederick wanted to do everything he could to support the Republican candidacy of a plain young man from Illinois named Abraham Lincoln.

The frontier lawyer had come to the country's attention when he opposed Stephen A. Douglas's insistence that each new territory should determine its slavery status. "The

Union cannot long endure half slave and half free,"[1] Lincoln had said. The country must choose one or the other, he insisted, and Lincoln himself believed that slavery would become extinct. "In a few simple words," Frederick later wrote, "he had embodied the thought of the loyal nation, and indicated the character fit to lead and guide the country amid perils present and to come."[2] The South eyed Lincoln with suspicion from that day forward.

The three candidates of the 1860 presidential race took three distinct stands on the all-encompassing question of slavery: John Breckenridge believed the Constitution protected the rights of slaveholders and allowed them to carry it into whatever new territories they chose; Stephen A. Douglas continued to promote territorial sovereignty; and Abraham Lincoln held that the federal government should discourage slaveholding in the South and forbid its spread to new territories.

Frederick filled his newspaper with editorials supporting Lincoln and dissecting the rhetoric of pro-slavery senators and campaigned every chance he got.

Breckenridge's supporters openly declared their states would secede from the Union if he were not elected. Northerners feared that Lincoln's election would destroy the country; many were not willing to risk that in order to abolish slavery. Stephen Douglas was accused of adjusting his stand according to the location of his speech. America's atmosphere was charged with anger and unrest.

Does Lincoln have a chance? Frederick wondered. *Is the country willing to take a strong stand against slavery?*

In November 1860 the voters answered with a victory for Lincoln.

Frederick hoped this would help stabilize the country. He even stated in the December issue of *Frederick*

Douglass's Monthly that he thought the Southern states would not leave the Union. Lincoln had never promised immediate emancipation for the slaves. His plans were slow, measured, and cautious, like the man himself. He would work willingly with the slaveholders, if they would work with him. If anything, Frederick believed, Lincoln was too patient; would he forget those who had trusted in his hatred of slavery?

But the South was in no mood for compromise.

Before Lincoln's inauguration in March, South Carolina seceded from the Union. Other Southern states rapidly followed suit.

"Peace in sixty days"—they believe that in Washington,[3] marveled Frederick. *They truly believe that this war will be over any day now.*

Even Lincoln, who slipped into Washington for his inauguration under death threats, initially sent only seventy-five thousand state militiamen to secure federal forts and arsenals in the South.

Frederick had firm faith in the character of Lincoln. But he feared that pressures from those Northerners who did not want to fight for the slaves' emancipation would force Lincoln away from freeing the slaves. Many only wanted to preserve the Union.

But Frederick continued to believe. Even when the secretary of state stated that slaves would not be freed, regardless of the war's outcome, even when Generals McClellan and Butler warned that Union troops would suppress a slave rebellion if it occurred, even when the Union refused to welcome black soldiers or protect black workers in military camps from white soldiers' resentment and harassment, even when Lincoln himself stated that blacks were the cause of the Civil War, Frederick continued to believe that the war would end slavery in the United States.

"Why do you fight the rebels with only one hand, when you might strike effectually with two?" asked Frederick. "You fight with your soft white hand, while you keep your black iron hand chained and helpless behind you."[4] Blacks, he asserted, had more reason to fight than anyone. The North was losing valuable, motivated soldiers by rejecting blacks. Finally the North armed their black laborers, but did not consider them true soldiers. Even their uniforms were different from those of white soldiers; the blacks wore red shirts. Blacks also received half the wages of white soldiers. Only white officers led them. Such treatment enraged Frederick, but he still worked tirelessly to encourage black men to enlist in the army. He helped Governor Andrew of Massachusetts raise two black regiments, the Fifty-fourth and Fifty-fifth, who fought bravely in North and South Carolina.

"Good-bye, Pa," said Lewis and Charles as they hugged Frederick at the train station. Frederick's own sons had enlisted in the Massachusetts regiments, since New York had none.

"Good-bye, *Father*," said Frederick, trying to hold back his tears, but determined as ever that his children would speak and act in an educated manner.

The boys grinned as they boarded the train. Frederick reminded himself that he would soon see them in Boston, when they officially joined their regiment before shipping out to Beaufort, South Carolina.

They look like children dressed in adult clothes. Merciful God, preserve my boys! Grant that Your cause will be accomplished soon before too many must die for it.

"The president will see you now," said the secretary.

Frederick took a deep breath. Lincoln must address the problems of black soldiers. Frederick had faced hecklers, fought in riots, and run for his life several times. He had met many famous people and learned not to be intimidated by the grand or powerful. But the prospect of meeting the president of the United States was still a little overwhelming.

Senator Pomeroy accompanied him to the little office where Lincoln sat in a low chair, long legs and big feet filling the room, surrounded by piles of documents and busy secretaries.

"Mr. President, I am Frederick Douglass, the editor of—"

"Yes, Mr. Douglass, I know who you are," Lincoln interrupted, his lined face breaking into a weary smile. "Mr. Seward has told me all about you. Please sit down! I am glad to see you and know your concerns. What, exactly, are they?"

"When I recruited black men as soldiers for the Union, I understood that they were to be treated as men," said Frederick. "I find this is not so, and I will not help raise any more regiments until it is."

"Are they mistreated?" asked Lincoln sharply. "In what way?"

Frederick cited examples that brought a flash of anger to the calm gray eyes. Some of the brave Massachusetts men had been captured and either tortured till they died or sold down South as slaves to the most notorious plantations. It was as if the usual humanitarian laws of warfare did not apply to blacks. Federal officials had not even protested. They made no effort whatsoever to exchange for black prisoners, as they did for white.

"My sons fight, and other black sons are fighting for their families and for this country, sir. Will their country refuse to protect them when they have proved their loyalty

179

in a thousand ways, risking their very lives for it?

"If Jefferson Davis should shoot or hang colored soldiers in cold blood, the United States government should, without delay, retaliate in kind and degree upon Confederate prisoners in its hands."[5]

Those who had acted valiantly in battle should also be rewarded as whites were, insisted Frederick. They should be subject to the same promotions, honors, and rewards that whites received.

Lincoln listened carefully and without comment until Frederick finished.

"I realize that prejudice against people of color is sadly prevalent in the North as well as the South," said the president. "That Negro troops are permitted to carry arms is progress I had not expected. I prefer greatly that they should be paid and honored equally, but I ask you—and them—to consider that such equality will only be accomplished gradually. It will, however, be accomplished."

Determination showed in his eyes. Frederick knew that Lincoln's opponents, who considered him an ignorant backwoods lawyer, underestimated the power of the man.

Lincoln went on to say that he could not agree to sentence Confederate prisoners to death simply because their leaders had acted unethically. "They personally were not involved in the torture and killings of black Northern prisoners. How can I hang men who are not overtly guilty? If we ourselves act as barbarians, where will it all stop?" He did, however, assure Frederick that the War Department had already begun to change its policies on prisoner exchanges; black prisoners, Lincoln declared, would be as eligible as white. He also would readily sign any black officers' commissions sent to him by the War Department.

When Frederick left, marveling at the amount of time

the president had devoted to their interview, he knew that they disagreed on several key points. But more than ever, Frederick believed in the integrity of the tired, lanky man in the White House.

Two years of the Civil War wore the Union down; Frederick himself felt threadbare and pessimistic. General George McClellan had accomplished little, Frederick felt; in two years of costly fighting, the Union had suffered defeat after defeat and barely held its ground. It was as if McClellan really did not want to win, only compel the rebels to rejoin the Union. Frederick also grew more and more impatient with Lincoln. "We have," he insisted, "a right to hold Abraham Lincoln sternly responsible for any disaster or failure attending the suppression of this rebellion."[6] He and several other antislavery speakers organized a well-publicized series of speeches at the Smithsonian Institution during the spring and summer of 1862. Their frequent message to the president was clear: the primary issue of this war is slave emancipation. Free the slaves, Mr. Lincoln!

To their amazement, the State Department finally announced in December 1862 that Lincoln had decided to issue an Emancipation Proclamation the next New Year's Day.

It is coming.

The words sounded in Frederick's head like a trumpet.

Jubilee is coming today, January 1, 1863.

Three thousand people, many of them black, packed Boston's Tremont Temple. A majority of them had been waiting all day. Surely the telegram would arrive any moment!

"We were waiting and listening as for a bolt from the sky, which should rend the fetters of four millions of slaves;

181

we were watching, as it were, by the dim light of the stars, for the dawn of a new day; we were longing for the answer to the agonizing prayers of centuries. Remembering those in bonds as bound with them, we wanted to join in the shout for freedom, and in the anthem of the redeemed," wrote Frederick later.[7]

William C. Nell, Anna Dickinson, and Frederick made brief speeches at Tremont Temple. Ralph Waldo Emerson, Harriet Beecher Stowe, and John Greenleaf Whittier spoke at the Boston Music Hall to an equally large crowd. The Boston Philharmonic played thunderous interludes of "Ode to Joy" once. . .twice. . .three times. Four.

Will jubilee come?

Lincoln might, at the last minute, decide that such a move was too radical. Members of Congress and Cabinet alike had pressured Lincoln against it since the beginning of the war. Northern racists might refuse to serve in the Union army if black slave emancipation was declared the war's goal. Could Lincoln afford to make this choice?

Will jubilee indeed come? Will it?

The people are heartsick. My comrades and I are doing our best to inspire them, but they have not gathered to hear good speeches. Ten o'clock, and still no word.

Will jubilee indeed come? Will it?

"IT IS ON THE WIRES!!" shouted Judge Thomas Russell. He plunged through the crowd, his face shining, clutching a paper in his hand. "IT IS COMING!"

But no one heard any more. Tremont Temple exploded into a chaos of joy; a thousand hats and bonnets soared skyward, and a multitude of voices rose in a chorus of joyful weeping and laughing.

"Let us sing our thanksgiving to the Almighty, for His mercy endures forever!" roared Rev. Rue, Frederick's old friend. The huge crowd vibrated with joy as they sang with his powerful baritone: "Sound the loud timbrel o'er Egypt's dark sea, Jehovah hath triumphed, his people are free."[8]

The people celebrated until midnight, then adjourned to Boston's Twelfth Baptist Church to rejoice until dawn. When the last choruses of "Glory, Hallelujah," had finally been sung by weary, blissful throats, Frederick made his way back to his hotel.

My eyes don't even want to close on this happy day, O God.

Not everyone rejoiced over the Emancipation Proclamation. Some abolitionists, on examining it more closely, declared it was limited severely by geographical and military boundaries. Although Frederick himself recognized the Proclamation's limitations, he chose to regard it as a precursor for the total cessation of slavery. It was the first step toward freeing slaves throughout all America and eventually winning them the privilege of citizenship and the vote. Lincoln, Frederick felt, was cautious, but had the integrity to carry through.

More troubling was the violence that erupted in several northern cities after the Proclamation. Enraged by the draft that exempted rich draftees for a price, poorer men vented their frustrations on those they regarded as the cause of the war: blacks. Riots broke out in New York in which whites attacked and hanged blacks simply because of their race. Some grabbed black women and children, smashing their heads against lamp posts and pavements. Two hundred black children ran for their lives when others burned down their orphanage. Black men, women, and children took refuge in cellars and attics, anywhere they could cower until the mob's rage was spent.

Frederick himself, on his way home from a recruiting mission in Philadelphia, was warned by Ottilia Assing of the ugly brawls, and managed to escape by a safer route.

Why are they so afraid of our freedom, God?

"Neither party," Lincoln said, "expected for the war the magnitude or the duration which it has already attained. Neither anticipated that the cause of the conflict might cease with or even before the conflict itself should cease. Each looked for an easier triumph and a result less fundamental and astounding."[9]

Frederick watched the president's second inaugural speech on the east portico of the Capitol with pride and relief. At one low point, Lincoln had despaired of victory in the South. He invited Frederick to the White House again to frame a plan in which enslaved blacks could escape to the North if he were forced to negotiate a peace with the Confederates in which blacks were not freed.

Frederick had replied with a plan similar to John Brown's Appalachian scheme.

But it was not needed, Frederick smiled to himself. At this moment, Grant and his forces were approaching Richmond, and Sherman was marching through Georgia. *With the victories in the South, Lincoln was re-elected. I am so thankful, O God. This country will need him more than ever.*

Frederick was aware, however, that not everyone in the smaller-than-usual crowds shared his satisfaction. The president openly labeled slavery as an affront to God, whose consequences the nation had experienced in the Civil War.

But Lincoln concluded, "With malice toward none, with charity for all, with firmness in the right as God gives us to see the right, let us strive to finish the work we are in, to bind up the nation's wounds, to care for him who shall have borne the battle, and for his widow and his orphans, to do all which may achieve and cherish a just and lasting peace among ourselves and with all nations."[10]

So much wisdom in such a brief speech. Frederick clapped his hands thankfully. Many applauded the president, who bowed slightly and waved.

Others stood stiffly, silent as the bare March trees.

"President Lincoln invited me and my guests to the inaugural reception, and I am going," said Frederick stubbornly. "Will no one accompany me?"

His black, prosperous friends smiled apologetically. Frederick glared at them; they fidgeted uncomfortably. They would love to go to the reception, Frederick knew. But, despite Lincoln's invitation, they knew their presence would be unwelcome. Blacks, wealthy or poor, were not accepted in Washington, D.C., society. Some blacks resented Frederick's boldness in asserting his rights, saying it only made more trouble for them. His friends celebrated it privately, but had no wish to humiliate themselves personally.

"Frederick, you will make a scene," said Albert Dickinson, a lawyer.

"Why should I make a scene?" asked Frederick. "I come at the invitation of my friend, the president of the United States. Shall I refuse such a momentous event in the name of timidity? I shall behave with all the propriety," Frederick grinned mischievously, "that the occasion demands."

His friends laughed. "You will make a scene," said Mrs. Thomas Dorsey, "but I will go with you."

"You! Go no farther!"

Two security guards flanked Frederick and Mrs. Dorsey

at the door of the White House. One grabbed Frederick's arm and tried to haul him away. He may as well have pulled on one of the pillars of the building; Frederick stood immovable, his muscular frame towering over the smaller man.

"What is the meaning of this?" said Frederick indignantly.

"No niggers in the White House," answered the policeman.

Frederick felt the familiar volcano erupt in his stomach, but he kept his tones measured. "Surely there must be some mistake," he said. "President Lincoln would have issued no such order." He edged forward to solidly block the entrance. Mrs. Dorsey followed suit.

The policemen exchanged glances. It would not do to confront such a man directly and disturb the president's party.

"Permit us to direct you," said the brighter of the two officers. He indicated a hallway to the right. Gratified, Frederick and Mrs. Dorsey walked through it, only to find themselves exiting out the side of the building!

"I will not leave this place until I see Mr. Lincoln," said Frederick furiously. He and his friend retraced their steps. Seeing an aide of the president's, Frederick accosted him before the irate policemen could eject them.

"Mr. Waddington, sir, would you be so kind as to tell Mr. Lincoln that Frederick Douglass is not permitted to enter?"

"Certainly, Mr. Douglass," he answered. The security guards looked at each other apprehensively. How could this black man know one of the president's people?

Waddington returned a few moments later, saying, "The president desires your immediate company, sir and madam."

Frederick bowed low to the two mortified officers, took Mrs. Dorsey's arm and followed Waddington. Hundreds of elegantly dressed guests wandered throughout the dazzling East Room. But Frederick had no problem spotting the president, who towered over the rest.

"Here comes my friend Douglass," beamed Lincoln. "I am glad to see you. I saw you in the crowd today, listening to my inaugural address; how did you like it?"

"Mr. Lincoln," said Frederick, "it was a sacred effort."

"I am glad you liked it!¹¹ Now, what was this difficulty you encountered at my door?"

"He was determined to look into it," said Frederick to Dickinson and his other friends at dinner a week later. "I was informed afterwards the guards had received no such orders from Lincoln. They had simply acted as in the past: 'no niggers allowed in the White House!' "

"It was a beautiful reception," said Mrs. Dorsey. "I have never seen such glittering chandeliers, such exquisite dresses and refreshment!" The other women sighed enviously.

"I will never forget my friend, the president," said Frederick.

It was the last time he would see Lincoln alive. One of the saddest addresses Frederick ever made was Lincoln's eulogy at a Rochester memorial service only a month later.

sixteen

e are free. We are free!
Frederick greeted every day with thanksgiving. No one was happier than he that slavery, the evil he had fought tirelessly with speeches, articles, and books, was finally dead.

But what shall I do now?

Frederick was no longer young. He had no immediate need to work in a brass foundry or candle and oil works, as he had in New Bedford. But he had ceased publishing his antislavery newspaper, and craved a new occupation. Frederick had saved proceeds from his book and lectures; perhaps he should consider buying a farm. The more he pondered, the more unsettled he became.

Financial considerations were important to Frederick, but they were not his only concerns. His days had been filled with meetings, lectures, travel, and socializing with antislavery advocates like himself. Now, many of Frederick's friends scattered far and wide. Like himself, they sought new beginnings. He missed the passion of his work, the joy of sharing it with others of like mind.

My true work is ended. My voice is no longer needed.

But many thought otherwise.

"A commencement address at Western Reserve College? Me?" said Frederick to his secretary. "I have never spent so much as a day in a schoolhouse. Why should they ask me?"

"Here are several more, Mr. Douglass," she answered. "Two commencement requests, a summer lecture series in New York City, and a dedication of a monument in Boston. They also mention," she said with a twinkle in her eye, "payment of one hundred to two hundred dollars per speech."

A flabbergasted Frederick continued to receive requests for his services. He had earned four hundred fifty dollars per year as a speaker for the Anti-Slavery Society, and felt well paid. Here was an amazingly profitable opportunity to study, speak, travel, and assist his newly-freed people!

For Frederick soon discovered, along with other blacks, that legal freedom did not necessarily mean true freedom. Many Southern masters, having lost sons, property, and privileges because of the Civil War, hated their former slaves and simply told them to leave the only homes they'd ever known. The slave "was free from the individual master, but the slave of society," wrote Frederick later. "He had neither money, property, nor friends. He was free from the old plantation, but he had nothing but the dusty road under his feet. He was free from the old quarter that once gave him shelter, but a slave to the rains of summer and to the frosts of winter. He was, in a word, literally turned loose, naked, hungry, and destitute to the open sky."[1]

Frederick also noted that racism in the North was as blatant as ever. Those who had lost loved ones in the war often blamed blacks, although they had fought and died as bravely as white soldiers. Resentment continued to simmer in industrial cities as whites and free blacks, many of whom had migrated north, competed for jobs. Predictably, blacks usually lost the battle in the workplace. They were no longer slaves, but they were not full citizens. The answer, Frederick believed, was granting them the right to vote.

The Negro still has a cause. He needs my voice and my pen, with others, to plead for it.[2] Frederick plunged into lecturing, writing, and campaigning for politicians who understood the necessity of black suffrage.

He also monitored President Andrew Johnson's Reconstruction policies.

Frederick and other black leaders, including his eldest son, Lewis, met with the president, hoping to discuss the roles of the newly freed slaves. Instead, Johnson spoke for forty-five minutes, refusing to allow them an answer to his address. Dismayed, the leaders asked Frederick to respond to the president in a letter that would be submitted to the newspapers.

"Believing as we do that the views and opinions you expressed in that address are entirely unsound and prejudicial to the highest interests of our race as well as to our country at large, we cannot do other than expose the same and, as far as may be in our power, arrest their dangerous influence," wrote Frederick.[3]

The black leaders worked tirelessly for the passage of an amendment that would grant their people the right to vote. Frederick's old Anti-Slavery Society friends joined the struggle, including Wendell Phillips. William Lloyd Garrison, with whom Frederick had reconciled earlier, was reluctant to support immediate black suffrage, but gradually threw his still-powerful influence behind the measure.

Blacks were uneducated and unfit to vote, the amendment's opponents insisted.

Frederick answered that this was a temporary situation. If this country grants the Negro the right to vote, he insisted, he will vote for more education for himself and become a better voter. Besides, Frederick declared, "If the Negro knows enough to fight for his country he knows enough to vote; if he knows enough to pay taxes for the support of the government, he knows enough to vote. . . ."[4]

Despite keen opposition, Frederick, his friends, and thousands of new voters celebrated the passage of the Fifteenth Amendment in 1870. Frederick was asked to speak to a huge, jubilant crowd in Baltimore.

I was a slave here, marveled Frederick. *I did not think I would ever return, unless it were in chains. Now I come here to shout aloud, "We can vote! We can vote!"*

"You can run for office, too," urged his friends. "Move to a black district in the South and run for office! You could be a senator!"

"If I were ten years younger," he told his eager supporters, "I would do it." But having served in public life for years, Frederick was not naïve enough to believe that such an undertaking would be simple!

He questioned whether even his closest white friends would support his candidacy for a congressional seat.

Too, it was time, Frederick reasoned, for the younger black men to take leadership. Perhaps some of their fiery, revivalist-type rhetoric would appeal more to the voters of the South. He himself had lived in New York for twenty years, and enjoyed a more measured style of oratory. He also disliked the idea of moving to a new area, ingratiating with strangers for their votes.

No, Frederick decided, *I believe I can do more for my people in my present vocations. When blacks are finally elected to Congress, it will be a long struggle before they have the audience and influence I have built over thirty years.*

Even though Frederick did not enter the official political arena, it was not long before he faced new challenges.

"Please come to Washington, D.C.," wrote George Downing, a prominent leader in black civil rights. "We need an experienced editor for the *New Era*. It is a weekly newspaper for our new voters, keeping them informed and granting them a forum to express their views."

A newspaper! Frederick groaned. Sixteen years of deadlines, financial pressures and sleep deprivation—that had been enough! But he could not say no. Newly enfranchised blacks needed information, *correct* information that would help them become better voters.

Frederick and his family moved to Washington, D.C., and Frederick threw himself into publishing once more, giving much of the day-to-day responsibilities of the paper to his sons, Lewis and Charles.

He campaigned extensively for Ulysses S. Grant, and continued to demand protection for black voters in the South, civil rights for the Chinese immigrants in the West, and suffrage for women. He served as secretary to President Grant's commission on the annexation of the Dominican Republic. It was a proud day for Frederick when, before the president, the Supreme Court, Congress, and thousands of others, he honored Abraham Lincoln at the dedication of the Freedmen's Monument, a statue erected by grateful black citizens.

The highest office Frederick Douglass ever achieved was that of U.S. Marshal of the District of Columbia, to which he was appointed by newly elected President Rutherford B. Hayes. Outraged whites stormed Hayes's office with protests; angry blacks insisted that Frederick's appointment was a mere sop to keep them quiet as Hayes conducted anti-black activities in the South. Frederick shrugged off objections on both sides, working hard at his job, enjoying the break from endless lecture tours, and using his position to gain government jobs for capable black friends.

"It has changed," said Frederick under his breath. "But, then again—not everything has."

St. Michaels, Maryland, was still a sleepy little town. Willow, Cherry, Cedar, Carpenter's Alley—the streets where he had shocked St. Michaels whites by carrying his head high back in the 1830s had not changed much. Neither had the names on the stores: Hambleton, Dawson, Dodson. But the weather-beaten houses now wore new coats of paint. A canning factory spoke of prosperity.

A black school stood at the edge of town.

What a shack, Frederick gritted his teeth. Obviously, the town fathers provided it only because the law demanded its existence. *But remember your Sunday school,* Frederick told himself. *Remember how they would not even permit children to learn the alphabet or the Scriptures. Now they must.*

He was glad to meet his sister Eliza's children and grandchildren, who welcomed him eagerly.

When the war was over, I went straight to Baltimore, Frederick remembered. *I saw Eliza there. It was as if Grandmammy Betsey threw her arms around me. She was just like her, so tall and dignified. But Eliza died last year, before I could make it back to visit her at St. Michaels.*

Frederick enjoyed his position as U.S. Marshal, but he grew tired of its political intrigues and paperwork. He felt a longing to return to Maryland, to the place of his birth and childhood.

Deep down, Frederick hoped to talk with his former owner, Thomas Auld.

He had vilified Thomas for decades, making him the personification of slave-owning evil in his speeches and writings. He had even written a blistering "Letter to My Old Master, Thomas Auld," published in the *North Star* in 1848, which contained not only his very valid grievances, but blame for offenses committed not by Auld, but by others, such as the vicious overseer Gore or the "slave-breaker," Covey.

"I have never forgotten you, but have invariably made you the topic of conversation—thus giving you all the notoriety I could do. . . .[5] I intend to make use of you as a weapon with which to assail the system of slavery. . .as a means of exposing the character of the American church and clergy—and as a means of bringing this guilty nation, with yourself, to repentance."[6]

In the letter, Frederick specifically blamed Captain Auld for his Grandmother Bailey's neglect. "My dear old grandmother, whom you turned out like an old horse to die in the woods—is she still alive? . . . Send her to me at Rochester, or bring her to Philadelphia, and it shall be the crowning happiness of my life to take care of her in her old age."[7]

Later Frederick had heard from reliable sources that Captain Auld had indeed cared for Grandmammy Betsey until her death.

Recently Frederick had also heard that Auld was quite elderly himself, and was failing fast.

Had he heard of Frederick's retraction in the *North Star* regarding Grandmammy Betsey? Auld had no way of knowing that Frederick, now approaching sixty himself, was beginning to question the vehemence with which he had attacked his former master.

The papers seem to follow my every move nowadays, thought Frederick. *Does Captain Auld know I am here in St. Michaels? Will anyone tell him?* He hardly felt at liberty to simply visit the man.

"If you please, Mr. Douglass," said a man at the edge of the crowd that had gathered on the arrival of the famous Frederick Douglass, "My name is Green. I am Captain Thomas Auld's servant. He requests the honor of your presence this afternoon at the home of his daughter, Mrs. William Bruff."

What will I say, O God?

"I gladly accept Captain Auld's invitation," Frederick answered formally. He followed Green to the corner of Cherry Lane and Locust Street.

The front door of the modest white house opened, and Louisa Bruff, Rowena Auld's daughter, met Frederick courteously. This in itself was enough to excite the crowd that had followed. No black man in St. Michaels had ever been invited to enter through the front door!

I can see Rowena in those tight lines around her mouth, Frederick thought, shuddering. *Those are her eyes, too.*

But the woman, despite her background, had evidently decided to honor her father's wishes.

"Mr. Douglass is here, Father," she said.

Frederick paused at the doorway.

"Captain Auld?"

"Marshal Douglass?" The pale, shaky old man in the bed struggled to sit up.

Did I expect to see Thomas Auld as he was forty-five years ago? Surely not! But this pitiful, sickly creature—was he the brutal master I so feared?

"I am not Marshal to you, Captain Auld," said Frederick gently. "Call me Frederick, as you did formerly." He paused. "How did you react when I ran away?"

A shadow of a smile played on the old man's face. "I always knew you were too intelligent to remain a slave, Frederick. If I had been in your place, I would have done the same."

"We were both victims of the slavery system," said Frederick grimly. "I was not escaping so much from you as from slavery itself." He paused awkwardly. "I want to apologize for having accused you of abusing my grandmother. I truly thought you had inherited her after Andrew Anthony's death and left her to die alone and helpless."

"I never owned Betsey," answered Thomas, with a trace of his old quickness. "But when I learned she was living by herself in the woods, I knew that would never do. She was too old. I brought her here and took care of her for the rest of her life.

"I never liked slavery," Thomas quavered. Tears ran down his emaciated cheeks, and he gripped Frederick's still-strong hand. "I planned to free all of my slaves when they turned twenty-five. I would have freed you, Frederick."

Silent forgiveness ran slowly, then, like a clear stream between them.

"When I see my Savior, as I soon shall, I can go in peace," said Thomas. "Thank you for coming to see me, Frederick. Good-bye." He leaned back on the pillow, exhausted by the effort he had made.

"Captain Auld, could you grant me one more request? I have never been certain of my birthday," said Frederick. "Tell me, sir, was I born in 1817 or 1818?" He felt a little silly, as if he were Freddy again.

"February 1818," answered Thomas with a faint grin.

"Thank you, Captain Auld," said Frederick, bowing to the old man and his daughter. He left, oblivious to the newspaper reporters who trailed after him. Their accounts stirred immediate controversy. Frederick Douglass, the great anti-slavery fighter had asked his former master to call him by his first name. Frederick Douglass, the great spokesman for black freedom, had groveled before his old master, asking forgiveness. Southern newspapers triumphantly pictured Frederick kneeling before Auld. Young blacks were up in arms; how could their hero behave in such a manner?

Frederick Douglass looked at his wealth, his literary and intellectual accomplishments, and his honored position, the highest any black man had yet achieved in the United States.

I will one day soon be in Thomas Auld's place. What will these things matter then, O God? I am thankful that our time of hatred is over.

seventeen

Encouraged by his trip to St. Michaels, Frederick returned to Maryland later to visit Tuckahoe Creek, the Lloyd Plantation, and even the jail in Easton, where he and his young co-conspirators had languished forty years before. Black critics attacked him for his ready reconciliation with the whites who had abused him; white racists ridiculed him. He ignored them all. Reminiscing with Colonel Lloyd's descendants, gathering an urn of earth from Grandmammy Betsey's cabin site to take back to his new estate, Cedar Hill, in Washington, D.C., thanking now eighty-year-old Easton Sheriff Joseph Graham for his humane treatment—Frederick found healing in all of these.

"I came to drink water from the old-fashioned well that I drank from many years ago, to see the few of the old friends that are left of the many I once had, to stand on the old soil once more before I am called away by the great Master, and to thank Him for His many blessings to me during my checkered life. . .that's all I came for," Frederick answered the reporters.[1]

He would need the serenity he had found in making peace with his past.

After much success, Frederick struggled for several years. His last and most elaborate autobiography, *Life and Times of Frederick Douglass,* did not sell well. James Garfield, the new president-elect, offered him the less prestigious job of county recorder. Some blacks who disagreed with his politics even booed him when he lectured. His children had numerous family problems; they always seemed to need extensive financial and emotional support. Frederick's siblings Perry and Kitty had, to his joy, reunited with him; but he found himself also supporting them when misfortune struck.

Worst of all, Anna's health, which had been fragile for years, worsened. Ottilia Assing, the German journalist who had remained Frederick's close friend for years, pressured him for more time and attention. Finally, Ottilia demanded he accompany her on a European tour. Frederick refused, remaining with his wife and family. Angered, Ottilia left the United States to live in Germany, where she grew more and more unstable.

In the summer of 1882 Anna suffered a stroke and died.

O Anna, I wish all our days together could have been like those at the first. Now you are gone. . . .

Black depression filled Frederick's life. He lost interest in his home, job, even politics. Alarmed, his doctor sent him with good friends Frank and Martha Greene to Poland Springs, Maine, a peaceful resort town. Refreshed, Frederick returned to a less strenuous schedule, but ready as ever to battle for black civil rights.

One day over a year after Anna's death, Frederick quietly summoned a clerk in his county recorder's office and obtained a marriage license. Later that January day in 1884 he married Helen Pitts, one of his employees.

Newspapers across the nation carried the shocking story. Frederick Douglass had married a white woman.

The new couple was not surprised at the notoriety that dogged them. They had expected such.

What they did not expect was the reaction of their families and close friends.

Frederick's grown children, unaware of his relationship with Helen, gave a hastily arranged reception for their father and his new wife, but they were aghast at his marriage. Helen's father, who had been a staunch abolitionist, refused to allow the Douglasses in his house. Black and white friends alike avoided socializing with them. Only a few, like Elizabeth Cady Stanton and Frederick's old English friend Julia Griffiths Crofts, wrote to congratulate the newlyweds. Ottilia Assing vilified Frederick in her letters to friends and committed suicide later that year, leaving her estate to him.

Frederick and the small, quiet, forty-five-year-old Helen enjoyed their time together, reading and attending lectures, the opera, and concerts. They often spent time playing piano/violin duets. The Douglasses traveled extensively throughout northern Europe, Egypt, and Greece.

Frederick's final years in the public arena were sometimes satisfying, often difficult. He and younger black leaders clashed regularly over political differences. Together, however, they denounced the Supreme Court's decision in 1883 which essentially disarmed the Fourteenth Amendment that had guaranteed equal rights to black U.S. citizens. Frederick celebrated his appointment at age seventy-one as consul general to Haiti, only to endure endless criticism because the United States did not procure its desired naval base there. He enjoyed his involvement in the World's

Columbian Exposition. It was a proud moment for Frederick when his grandson, Joseph Douglass, a concert violinist, performed at the Exposition.

As always, Frederick spoke, dedicating monuments, campaigning for candidates, and demanding an end to the lynchings and violence at the polls that had become commonplace in the South. He also continued to speak out for women's rights.

On the morning of February 20, 1895, Frederick, escorted to the podium by Susan B. Anthony, made a speech to the National Council of Women in Washington, D.C. He ate dinner with Helen; then, as the two waited for their carriage to take them to a church meeting, he entertained her with an elaborate imitation of a pretentious speaker he had heard that day. Helen's laughter turned to panic as Frederick suddenly slipped to the floor.

The mighty spokesman for freedom was dead of heart failure at age seventy-seven.

"The Lord has a great work for you to do," Uncle Lawson had once told the boy Frederick. "Trust in the Lord! All things are possible with Him, only *have faith in God!*"

Thousands of black children filed past Frederick's open casket in the Metropolitan African Methodist Episcopal Church.

None of them were slaves.

All had the opportunity to go to school.

All were United States citizens who would one day have the right to vote.

Like Frederick, they would face prejudice and difficulty on every side. But because he helped blaze the trail for their freedom, the road to Canaan was in sight.

Sources

Douglass, Frederick. *Life and Times of Frederick Douglass*. Autobiographies. Ed. by Literary Classics of the United States. New York: Library of America, 1994 [1893].

My Bondage and My Freedom. Autobiographies. Ed. by Literary Classics of the United States. New York: Library of America, 1994 [1855].

Narrative of the Life of Frederick Douglass, an American Slave. Autobiographies. Ed. by Literary Classics of the United States. New York: Library of America, 1994 [1845].

Huggins, Nathan Irvin. *Slave and Citizen: The Life of Frederick Douglass*. Boston: Little, Brown and Company, 1980.

McFeely, William. *Frederick Douglass*. New York: W. W. Norton and Company, 1991.

Preston, Dickson J. *Young Frederick Douglass: The Maryland Years*. Baltimore: Johns Hopkins University Press, 1980.

Quarles, Benjamin. *Frederick Douglass*. New York: Atheneum, 1969 [1948].

Notes

Chapter 1

[1]Frederick Douglass. *My Bondage and My Freedom.*
Autobiographies. Ed. by Literary Classics of the
United States. (New York: Library of America,
1994 [1855]), 148.

[2]Ibid.

[3]Ibid., 149.

[4]Ibid., 180.

[5]Ibid., 178.

[6]Frederick Douglass. *Narrative of the Life of
Frederick Douglass, an American Slave.*
Autobiographies. Ed. by Literary Classics of the
United States. (New York: Library of America,
1994 [1845]), 18.

Chapter 2

[1]Douglass, *Bondage,* 155.

[2]Douglass, *Narrative,* 24.

[3]Douglass, *Bondage,* 194.

[4]Ibid., 213.

Chapter 4

[1]Douglass, *Bondage,* 231.

[2]Ibid.

[3]Ibid., 233.

Chapter 5

[1]Frederick Douglass. *Life and Times of Frederick
Douglass.* Autobiographies. Ed. by Literary
Classics of the United States. (New York:
Library of America, 1994 [1893]), 554.

Chapter 6

[1]Douglass, *Bondage,* 268.
[2]Ibid.
[3]Ibid., 268–69.
[4]Douglass, *Life,* 601.

Chapter 8

[1]Douglass, *Narrative,* Appendix, 99–100.
[2]Douglass, *Bondage,* 336–37.
[3]Ibid., 344.

Chapter 9

[1]Douglass, *Life,* 645.
[2]Ibid., 647.
[3]Ibid., 649.

Chapter 10

[1]Douglass, *Life,* 653.
[2]Ibid.
[3]Ibid., 654.
[4]Douglass, *Bondage,* 360.
[5]Douglass, *Life,* 658.
[6]Ibid.
[7]Ibid., 659.

Chapter 11

[1]From *Frederick Douglass* by William S. McFeely.
Copyright © 1991 by William S. McFeely.
Reprinted by permission of W. W. Norton &
Company, 88–9.
[2]Douglass, *Life,* 661.
[3]Ibid.
[4]Ibid., 670.

[5]Ibid., 668.
[6]Douglass, *Narrative,* Appendix, 97.
[7]Douglass, *Bondage,* Appendix, 407.
[8]Douglass, *Narrative,* Appendix, 97–8.
[9]Ibid., 100.

Chapter 12
[1]Douglass, *Life,* 689.
[2]Ibid., 695.
[3]Ibid., 686.
[4]Ibid., 699.
[5]Ibid., 700.

Chapter 13
[1]Douglass, *Life,* 662.
[2]Ibid., 710.

Chapter 14
[1]Douglass, *Bondage,* Appendix, 431.
[2]Ibid., 431–32.
[3]Ibid., 434.
[4]Douglas, *Life,* 719.
[5]Ibid.
[6]Ibid., 720.
[7]Ibid., 719.
[8]Ibid., 760.

Chapter 15
[1]Douglass, *Life,* 737.
[2]Ibid.
[3]Ibid., 774.
[4]Ibid., 775.
[5]Ibid., 786.

[6]McFeely, 214.

[7]Douglass, *Life,* 791.

[8]Ibid., 792.

[9]Ibid., 801.

[10]Ibid., 801–2.

[11]Ibid., 804.

Chapter 16

[1]Douglass, *Life,* 815.

[2]Ibid., 816.

[3]Ibid., 821.

[4]Ibid., 819.

[5]Douglass, *Bondage,* Appendix, 415.

[6]Ibid., 418.

[7]Ibid., 417.

Chapter 17

[1]Dickson J. Preston, *Young Frederick Douglass: The Maryland Years* (Baltimore: Johns Hopkins University Press, 1980), 197.

HEROES OF THE FAITH

This exciting biographical series explores the lives of famous Christian men and women throughout the ages. These trade paper books will inspire and encourage you to follow the example of these "Heroes of the Faith" who made Christ the center of their existence. 208 pages each. Only $3.97 each!

Gladys Aylward, Missionary to China

Dietrich Bonhoeffer,
Opponent of the Nazi Regime

Brother Andrew, God's Undercover Agent

Corrie ten Boom, Heroine of Haarlem

William and Catherine Booth,
Founders of the Salvation Army

John Bunyan,
Author of *The Pilgrim's Progress*

William Carey, Father of Missions

Amy Carmichael, Abandoned to God

George Washington Carver,
Inventor and Naturalist

Fanny Crosby, the Hymn Writer

Frederick Douglass,
Abolitionist and Reformer

Jonathan Edwards, the Great Awakener

Jim Elliot, Missionary to Ecuador

Charles Finney, the Great Revivalist

Billy Graham, the Great Evangelist

C. S. Lewis, Author of *Mere Christianity*

Eric Liddell, Olympian and Missionary

David Livingstone, Missionary and Explorer

Martin Luther, the Great Reformer

D. L. Moody, the American Evangelist

Samuel Morris,
the Apostle of Simple Faith

George Müller, Man of Faith

Mother Teresa, Missionary of Charity

Watchman Nee, Man of Suffering

John Newton, Author of "Amazing Grace"

Florence Nightingale,
Lady with the Lamp

Luis Palau, Evangelist to the World

Francis and Edith Schaeffer,
Defenders of the Faith

Charles Sheldon, Author of *In His Steps*

Mary Slessor, Queen of Calabar

Charles Spurgeon, the Great Orator

John and Betty Stam, Missionary Martyrs

Billy Sunday, Evangelist on Sawdust Trail

Hudson Taylor,
Founder, China Inland Mission

Sojourner Truth, American Abolitionist

William Tyndale,
Bible Translator and Martyr

John Wesley, the Great Methodist

George Whitefield, Pioneering Evangelist

Available wherever books are sold.
Or order from:
Barbour Publishing, Inc.
P.O. Box 719
Uhrichsville, Ohio 44683
http://www.barbourbooks.com

If you order by mail, add $2.00 to your order for shipping.
Prices subject to change without notice.